A WALK THROUGH LEADERSHIP

DARROCH "ROCKY" YOUNG

ISBN: 0615866212
ISBN 13: 9780615866215

Library of Congress Control Number: 2013915152
Seaway Publishing
Port Ludlow, WA

This book is dedicated to my wife Diane who stood outside the limelight while she provided me with the support that made it possible for me to have a successful personal and professional life. But most importantly she provided me with an endless supply of energy, enthusiasm and encouragement because of her unwavering belief in me and my leadership ability.

About the Author

Darroch "Rocky" Young retired as Chancellor of the Los Angeles Community College District on July 31, 2007. In his retirement, he has worked as the Chief Consultant for the College Brain Trust (CBT). He has provided consulting on strategic planning to numerous colleges including College of Western Idaho (ID), Oakland Community College (MI), West Valley-Mission Community College District (CA), Grossmont-Cuyamaca Community College District (CA), Rancho Santiago Community College District (CA), MiraCosta College (CA) and Citrus College (CA). Furthermore, for the last four years Rocky has been working for the California Community College League for California by running their annual New CEO Workshop and the annual Vineyard Symposium (for experienced CEOs) in Napa Valley.

As Chancellor, Rocky initiated the first formal Comprehensive Strategic Planning effort in the District's history and dramatically improved the District's financial condition. Rocky also launched a major Student Success Initiative that aimed at improving all student educational outcomes across the District—including student graduation, transfer, and job placement rates. Chancellor Young initiated an aggressive district-wide marketing campaign to publicize community college educational opportunities and revamped the District's enrollment management programs. He also initiated a district-wide leadership development program (ALP).

Before assuming district-wide responsibilities, Rocky Young was President of Pierce College, a position he took in 1999. Under his leadership, the college increased its enrollment by 51% in less than 3 years, making it the fastest growing community college in California. He put a Master Plan in place that included extensive community involvement, created a new 15-week semester plan that has become the most copied academic calendar in California and reversed years of financial difficulties to create healthy financial reserves for the college. In addition, Young fostered new partnerships with Caltech, UCLA, UC Berkeley and CSUN, as well as a number of industry partners in the private sector. Young also created strong alliances for the college with neighborhood groups, businesses, and elected officials.

Prior to coming to Pierce College, Rocky Young served as Vice President of Academic and Student Affairs and Vice President of Planning and Development at Santa Monica College where he created the concept for the Santa Monica College Academy of Entertainment and Technology, formed partnerships with fifty entertainment firms, and led the effort to receive the Board of Governors approval of the Academy as an educational center. In addition, he created the Transfer Alliance Program with UCLA, developed a high school dual enrollment program with local unified school districts, and created the College's first Master Plan for Education, Comprehensive Facilities Master Plan, and the Master Plan for Technology.

Rocky was awarded the 2007 Harry Buttimer Award as the outstanding community college executive in California, the 2003 Pacesetter of the Year by the National Council of Marketing and Public Relations, the 2003 Steve Allen Award for Excellence in Education, and the 1998 ACCCA Leadership Award for Administrative Excellence in California Community Colleges.

Table of Contents

❖

Introduction

W hen I retired after spending over 36 years in the community college system, I was fortunate enough to be
invited on a number of occasions to speak to groups
about various aspects of leadership. In preparing those remarks,
and in reflecting over my different leadership positions, I was always presented with a series of dilemmas. Can anyone dissect the
development of leadership skills into those created by life experience, those that are an extension of one's personality and those
that were taught by someone else? I know from my own career that
all three were important.

This book is aimed at leaders and potential leaders at a community college (administrators, faculty, staff and students) but
most of these principles are universal and would be applicable for
any leadership situation. No matter what leadership situation you
face, I think there are new skills that can be taught to current and
future leaders. Since everyone has a unique mix of life experiences
and personality characteristics, everyone is at a different place in
his or her leadership development. However, there are always some
additional critical leadership skills that can be taught regardless of
a person's unique background and experience.

I also wanted to avoid my frustration with many treatises on
leadership in which a concept was amplified beyond reason. Too
often, in leadership books, an entire chapter is presented on a

concept that only needs one page. You can see by the length of this book that I have tried not to do that. Because the book is relatively short, the reader could probably finish the entire book in one sitting. However, since the hard part for me in using leadership books is the integration of the content into my leadership style, the book probably lends itself to being read (or reread) in small doses and allowing for that integration to occur.

Another disappointment I have had with leadership books is that they tend to be very dry and make very little effort to help the reader internalize the concepts. To help the reader overcome this problem, the book has been written as a narrative and a dialogue in a spirit similar to *"Tuesdays With Morrie."* The first part of the book is a series of discussions between a woman embarking on a leadership position and her retired grandfather who had years of experience as they take walks together. The second part continues those discussions and those walks later in the woman's career as she is about to assume the role of college president. The relationship is not critical, but I thought the dialogue helped to make the material more readable.

No matter where you are in your leadership career, I hope you will read the entire book. The leadership skills discussed in the first half of the book are as critical to a college president as anything discussed in the second half of the book. Conversely, for those just assuming their first leadership position, you will find value in the discussions of the second half of the book. In the end, leadership skills do not fall into two distinct parts. Rather, virtually all leadership skills are applicable to some degree in every leadership situation.

The ultimate goal is to have the reader internalize the skills discussed in the book, so I also tried to create some skill metaphors within the story. As a reader of other leadership books, I quickly forgot the "list of critical skills" before I ever internalized any of them, especially because the process of internalization takes time.

I thought familiar metaphors might help the reader to remember the skills. The difficulty is finding metaphors for all ages. You will notice in the movie and television metaphors that they are the most memorable to my age group but hopefully they are "classics" and transcend all age groups. In any event, if you find other metaphors that work better for you, use them. It is important to make the skill being discussed memorable to you, and any metaphor that works for you should be substituted.

Another important part of internalization is to be constantly reminded of the skills you are trying to incorporate. To help you, I have provided some brief summaries of those skills at the end of each chapter or in tables within the chapter. Readers can easily copy these pages for quick reference and add their own notes to those from the book.

Before you read this book, I want to discuss my distinction between leadership skills and managerial skills. I have always thought of managerial skills as those skills necessary to successfully maintain and operate the institution. There has never been any doubt that these skills can be learned and many of them are primarily informational in nature. Developing the skills to critically analyze operational situations is more challenging but is really just knowing the relevant information and using one's critical thinking skills.

It is also important to recognize that the line between leadership skills and managerial skills is fuzzy and arbitrary. However, I have always felt that mastering managerial skills was a necessary, but not a sufficient, condition to being a successful leader. Another importance of understanding and acquiring managerial skills is that whenever a leader does not possess them, he or she is dependent on someone else within the organization. That may be a problem because it makes the leader vulnerable. At a minimum it means that the leader cannot actively participate in discussions on the subject and cannot help to develop a strategy for dealing with a problem situation. Worse yet, if the organization does not have someone with the necessary skills, there is a huge hole in organizational operations. For people who are still ascending within the organization, ideally they will acquire managerial skills while they develop the leadership skills discussed in this book. A person who has mastered managerial skills but not developed the necessary leadership skills may be a capable person to maintain the status quo of an organization. Unfortunately, an organization cannot survive and prosper by maintaining the status quo, but instead will begin to wither and die.

To lead the organization in new directions and to new heights requires that the leader has also mastered leadership skills. This book exclusively focuses on those leadership skills which must supplement managerial skills. A leader absolutely needs to have the managerial skills because an organization that is not operating properly cannot grow and achieve a new vision. So don't neglect mastery of managerial skills but look for other sources to learn them (a partial list of important managerial skills is provided in the Appendix).

Developing leadership skills is a continuous journey throughout one's career and is not something acquired by a simple "inoculation" of information. I hope you find my reflections useful. I also hope you find this book to be an easy, enjoyable read so that you will revisit it at various appropriate times during your leadership journey. Good luck and I hope you are successful because this world desperately needs more skilled leaders.

I would be remiss if I did not acknowledge the help I received in writing this book. I would like to thank Diane Young for her work as my copy editor, John Spevak for his help in editing the content and presentation of the book, and Eva Conrad and Suzie Chock Hunt for their input and encouragement. I would also like to thank Anthony Pitassi for the book's cover design. Even more importantly, I would like to thank everyone who has helped me develop my leadership skills during my own leadership evolution.

LEARNING TO CLIMB

❖

1

Finding the Path

One of my favorite times is to be in my office on a Friday evening when the sun is setting but it is still light and almost everyone has gone home. My office is no executive suite and, in fact, it is barely able to hold my office partner and me. The office is only long enough to house two old wooden single pedestal desks sitting side-by-side and only wide enough for us to get in and out of our old wooden swivel desk chairs. When my office partner is at his desk, our office is so small that it is hard to maneuver past the back of his chair to get to my desk. However, I am really the lucky one because he chose the desk by the door so I get the desk by the window. At this time of day, looking out that window is wonderful – especially when I am alone. There is a glorious deciduous tree right outside the window that perfectly reflects the seasons of the year, and past it I can look out at the grass quad with its beautiful trees surrounding the historic clock tower.

The college has frequently offered to replace my old wooden office furniture with new metal furniture but I always turn them down. I feel as if my old desk connects me with my faculty predecessors. I even enjoy the unintended stray marks from an old pen or the nicks created by an accidental encounter with a sharp object. These feelings for my old desk are really just an extrapolation of my private, professional passion for the history of the college. Wherever I work, I want to feel connected, both to the present and the past.

Since I am the faculty member with the least seniority in the department, I teach all over campus in any available spare classroom. Most faculty hate when this happens to them because they want to teach in immediate proximity to their office. But that is not who I am. I like teaching in multiple locations. It is particularly fun when I teach in the oldest building on campus and realize that it was used for training during World War II, or in the old administration building with its history of civil rights and anti-war demonstrations in the 1960s. I like walking past the spot where a gay man was crowned as the first male homecoming queen. None of these connections would have happened for me without my passion for the history of the college. And, even that passion would not have meant anything without my befriending the head librarian who allows me to explore the college archives in my spare time.

As usual, when I sit in my office at this time of day, my mind wanders. I realize that it is probably foolish for a 27-year-old woman to be sitting alone in her office on a somewhat deserted college campus, but there are times I am not going to let fear rule my life. I have always been strong willed with a mind of my own or I would not have ended up here at this point in my life. However, even that is an unusual story. I was always a good, but not exceptional or great, student until I started graduate school. For some reason, for the first time in my life, I decided to "give it my all" and the results astounded me. Probably because of these grad school achievements, my professors (and to some extent my peers) were dismayed when I told them at graduation that I was going to be a community college faculty member. The more charitable ones said it was "noble" while the less charitable called it a waste of my talents. Frankly, I was amazed at how so many intelligent, educated people used a television sitcom stereotype of community colleges as an accurate representation.

Of course, if you knew me, you would know that I followed my passion to teach lower division undergraduates and ignored all of the remarks from within the university. In spite of all this commentary, I knew there was one person who was thrilled – my grandfather. I knew he would never say anything to try to influence my career decisions and he would support whatever decision made me happy. However, as a former community college president and avid supporter of community colleges, he secretly loved the idea that I was becoming a part of a community college. By serendipity, it even became better because the college that offered me a tenure-track job was his former college. Of course, by the time I arrived at the college, most of his peers were gone and even his memory was just a name on a plaque on the wall. Because our last name is so common, the people who hired me would not have made the connection even if they had remembered him.

During the four years that I have worked at the college I have never mustered up the courage to ask anybody about my grandfather. In terms of my career, I did not want anyone to know about the relationship because I did not want them to think I was hired or promoted because of him. I wanted to be sure, both in my mind and in the minds of others, that all of my achievements were on my own merits. My other anxiety had to do with my grandfather. He never talked with me about his time as president; so I worried that he was unsuccessful or, worse yet, something bad had happened.

Last week I finally decided that it was silly to avoid knowing about my grandfather, so I took one of the kindly old-timers into my confidence, explained the relationship and asked about my grandfather's time at the college. He laughed about both of my concerns. He said that there were so few people left from his era that he doubted that I could derive any favored treatment from anyone at the college, but he would keep the information of the relationship to himself. More importantly, he said my grandfather had been one of the most successful presidents in the history of the college. He went on to say that he was well liked and people were sad to see him retire; so I did not need to be afraid to "turn over that rock". As you might guess, I made a beeline for the archives and resurrected the old school newspapers from his time on campus. The information I had been told was correct. Grandpa was credited with turning around the college by taking it from one of its darkest moments and helping to lead it to prosperity and eminence. The newspaper called it the "renaissance" of the college.

What I am really thinking about as I stare out my office window is that I have just reached another junction in my life. I just finished my fourth year at the college and I have earned tenure. This was my personal minimum commitment to this job when I accepted it. But I have never had one moment of regret over making this career decision and I plan to stay for the foreseeable future. However, that is only part of it. I was just elected department chair. This was a dramatic change from tradition in which the chair was usually the most senior member of the department who sought the job. As a woman, I am not concerned about my gender being a problem because I have had other women precede me within the department and there are numerous other women department chairs at the college.

I am a little worried, however, about my age being a problem. I will be by far the youngest department chair at the college. However, my greater concern is that I am the youngest member of the department and I will have the responsibility of leading a group of people who are both more experienced than me and at least 15 years older than me. I am confident in my abilities, but I hope my age doesn't become an unstated obstacle with any of my colleagues. It was truly an honor to be elected, but now I need to develop the leadership skills to meet their expectations. How will I do that? The good news is that the college is just ending its spring semester, and I don't assume my duties as department chair until the fall. I am teaching just one class in the summer so I have time to prepare for this new assignment.

With the onset of summer I use my usual strategy for attacking a new challenge by going to our local bookstore and buying all of the books on leadership that look interesting. However, after reading through a half-dozen books, I became frustrated. Many of the books took a whole chapter to discuss a concept that could have been described in one paragraph. Others were really nothing more than a list of leadership traits. I realized that they were useless unless I could internalize them or find some way to remember them. I know that my grandfather always told me that becoming a leader was a slow process of acting as a leader, reflecting on your performance, and altering your behavior based on your mistakes (or reinforcing your successes). He said it was like eating a nine-course meal, one mouthful at a time. Unfortunately, I was being thrust into this role immediately and I did not have the time to digest "my leadership meal". So, when I get frustrated, I eat a piece of dark chocolate (a leadership appetizer) and go do something that is fun. For me, I thought it might be fun to go talk to my grandfather.

My grandfather and I have always had a very loving relationship, but I cannot say that we ever discussed anything in depth. He is a very kind and gentle man who rarely talks about himself or his past. Besides this genuine modesty and lack of egocentricity, he does not live very close to me so it is an effort for us to get together. That has come to mean that we primarily see each other at holidays with all of the other family members present. Not exactly a conducive setting for a meaningful discussion. Besides he always directs the conversation to me and what I am doing. I only have vague memories of going to the college with him when he was president, and even then it was always my desire to go to the agriculture department and see the animals. Combined with his reticence to discuss his past, the fact that he retired before I started teaching, also made our conversations about his community college presidency a rarity. Nevertheless, I decided it was worth a try.

When I arrived at grandpa's house, I was greeted with the usual smile and loving hug, although he was surprised to see me. After I assured him that there was nothing wrong with me or mom or dad or anyone else in the family, we immediately moved to our common bond of a love for dark chocolate and dove into some Valrhona Chocolate that he had received as a gift. I finally got around to why I had come and told him that I wanted him to help me learn to be a successful community college leader like he had been. I told him what the "old timer" and newspapers had said. They called him a very successful community college president. As usual, grandpa was dismissive of the idea that he had something to teach me; but after continuing to push him, he started to relent.

Before I tell you about all of the subsequent conversations, it is important to realize that we were about to change the nature of our relationship. Grandpa had always been a rather traditional grandfather. We didn't see each other that often and he was always somewhat distant but in a very loving way. I think he always felt that his role was just to provide unconditional love but that he had no responsibility for raising me or teaching me – he left that completely to my parents. Now, I was asking him to be a colleague and a mentor. I could see his reluctance to change our relationship (perhaps because he would have to reveal a lot more about himself and his life to me). Nevertheless, he did finally seem willing to at least start down the path.

"If we are going to talk about my time as a community college president," grandfather said, "I want to start at the end, not the beginning." The end was his retirement celebration. He recognized when he retired that he relished recognition as much as anyone. In fact, he understood how genuine appreciation of his efforts meant the world to him. But, he also learned the difference between genuine and ceremonial recognition. There are very few items in his house which would ever allow you to know that he had been a college president. No pictures with celebrities or framed proclamations on the walls. The few items that were out were the ones that he said really mattered because they came from the people who knew him and worked with him – the students, the faculty, the classified employees, the managers, the trustees and most importantly, his leadership team.

"The reason that these are the people that matter," grandfather said, "is because leadership is a team sport. The recognitions that matter are the ones that come from your team. The leader gets the recognition (and the blame) from people external to the team, but success only occurs through the combined effort of the team."

"You might be on point 'picking the path with your lantern,'" he explained, "but you'd better have people following you and you had better have people to help you do the heavy lifting when the time comes for action. That is why recognition from the team is so meaningful because they know whether success was because of you or in spite of you. Usually leaders run aground when they start to think that leadership is an individual sport and if that happens, you are no longer a leader."

To punctuate his point, grandfather showed me what he calls his "ceremonial memorial closet". It is packed with beautifully framed proclamations that express wonderful sentiments about his professional accomplishments. He said there is a wonderful set of ironies regarding the contents of the closet. On the one hand, he would have been deeply hurt if he hadn't received all of these documents because he knew from attending retirement functions for his peers that this is the typical rite of passage for a leader's retirement. On the other hand, he is not naïve. He knows that these commendations are boiler plate documents in which someone else supplies the relevant information for insertion. I had awarded some of these commendations, he said, to others that were constructed in the same manner. If that wasn't enough, he now had to decide what to do with them. Even if I wanted to, he said, Grandma would never let me turn our house into a personal shrine. She always said it was her job to keep me humble by having me take out the trash and clean the toilets!

When he walks by the closet, he does appreciate that the ceremonial gifts were gracious acts by the givers, but they are not his definition of recognition and success. With his usual sense of humor, he said, "I always wanted to create an alternative form of recognition. Proclamations should be prepared as labels that can be affixed to a really nice bottle of wine. One of the retirement gifts could be a proclamation wine rack. Then, at appropriate times, retirees could drink one of the bottles, read the proclamation and have a lovely reflection on their careers as they sip the wine. They would then return the empty to the wine rack so in the future they could remember both the words and the wine." Grandpa said, "Putting all my kidding aside, I did receive a few naming honors which I will always cherish, because the recognition felt genuine, unique and long-lasting."

While grandpa had taught me my first important lesson - leadership is a team sport - I realized that this was not going to be easy to extract leadership wisdom from him. We had spent most of the time talking about the ironies of retirement celebrations rather than how he had success as a leader. I think this was another diversion by grandpa to turn attention away from himself. Nevertheless, I was grateful that we had crossed the threshold and that grandpa was willing to talk about his past. Even though we did not make much progress today, we did agree to meet again next week.

❖

2

Mapping the Walk

For our second meeting, I agreed to meet grandpa at his favorite seafood restaurant overlooking the ocean. He never seems to tire of spending time on the beach and near the ocean. It always energizes him and today was no exception. He was already in a booth by the window waiting for me and enjoying the whole atmosphere. After he talked to me about the cormorants and pelicans (two birds he loved to watch fish), along with his disappointment with the shore break of the waves (which harkened back to his time in the surf in his youth), he was ready to order his food. Grandpa ordered one of his favorites, a fresh crab sandwich on fresh sourdough bread with cole slaw. I had my favorite which was a fresh salmon sandwich with mango chutney and French fries. We both had a diet soda with our lunch. We exchanged pleasantries while waiting for our food, but grandpa had obviously thought about today's lunch and seemed ready to talk about his past. As the food arrived, he started talking.

> I appreciated that you heard good things about my time as president of the college, but I learned that if you are going to be reflective about your

performance as a leader, you need to have some standard to measure against that performance. That means you must have some internal sense of success. The measure must be internal because a leader doesn't ever want to chase external approval. If leaders ever start to make decisions to generate approval from others, they are now following rather than leading. That sounds simple and logical but approval is an intoxicating elixir. Everyone wants to be liked and to receive accolades. However, that needs to be a by-product of leadership and not an influencing factor. This is even a bigger issue when you recognize that with every new leadership position you gain "friends" who are trying to self-promote and trying to influence decisions for their benefit (either directly or indirectly by demonstrating to others their influence on you). Besides, even legitimate friends cannot be allowed to use that friendship to affect decisions. The need for an internal calibration of what is right and what defines success, along with a wariness of friendships, is an important recognition for someone starting the leadership trail. Because being a leader requires maintaining an emotional distance from others, it can, by necessity, be lonely.

Most of your support will come from your "superiors" who will be evaluating your performance and from your peers (people in comparable positions) with whom you will share common experiences without being in each other's area of influence.

Grandpa went on say, "I am not trying to scare you, but at times people don't realize the personal limitations imposed on leaders.

The biggest issue will be the potential burden imposed on personal relationships and your family. There is no leadership position that is ever finished and there is never a time when leaders have to worry about what to do with their free time at work. This places an enormous pressure on you to determine your boundaries."

Grandpa said that he felt one of his failings as a leader was that he did not set those boundaries properly – especially with regard to spending more time with his children. He was raised with the belief that a person had a primary obligation to fulfill his professional responsibilities above all else. This was partially a consequence of being raised in a very traditional family with a stay-at-home mother who was charged with raising the children and a father who put work first. Grandpa replicated that behavior.

> When you work all the time, you get enormous praise from everyone around you at work, and your family tends to accept it as the reality of your job. Yet, it means you spend less time with all of your relationships and you neglect your involvement in activities outside of work. As you progress up the "leadership ladder," the time demands become greater and the job becomes more isolating. That is why I feel it is important to determine these boundaries at the outset because as you are promoted you tend to repeat your prior behaviors or exaggerate them if you feel they caused your success. You also need to continually revisit the question of boundaries as your life changes (you get married, you have children) and the amount of time you have remained in the same position. All leadership positions require more time at the outset, but if you don't revisit the boundary question, you will simply expand the job to the available hours as you gain maturity in the job. You also

need to assess your productivity by asking whether spending 12 hours a day instead of spending 10 hours a day is really making a significant and meaningful difference.

"And," grandpa said, "here is the real lesson of experience. I am not sure that all of that extra time actually added enough to justify the cost!"

Consistent with finding balance in one's life and finding balance between work and personal life, it is also important to know what makes you happy. Successful leaders will be encouraged by followers, peers and superiors to assume new leadership positions with greater responsibility. The desire to promote you is wonderful praise of your abilities and it can cause you to seek those positions. Furthermore, you will not really know if you would enjoy these positions until you perform them. Nevertheless, I have a series of cautions for you. If at all possible, have a plan. It is incredibly useful if people know their ultimate (or even their short-term) goal. There are many opportunities that will be presented to you which may not represent your desired destination but they will help you to achieve your goal.

"Also," grandpa said, "I always tried as many different opportunities as possible because I always learned something new in each position and each inevitably helped me sometime during my career."

On the other hand, if you are content in a position, don't feel compelled to abandon it just because a promotion pays more or has more prestige. Every leadership position is important within its own sphere of influence and being "higher" in the organization is not necessarily better. Many people have paid a lot of attention to the "Peter Principle" which refers to people being promoted beyond their abilities. However, that is an organizational problem of selecting the wrong person. For you, there is a more important principle. You may be incredibly successful and competent at doing a job, but you are not happy. Too many people assume that competence and success equate with professional happiness. That is not necessarily true. It is hard to be happy when a person is not competent or successful, but the opposite is not necessarily true. Remember that so that you don't stay locked into a job you do very well but don't like.

This brought grandpa to his final point on this subject – "it is okay to quit a job." While he recommended that people should always line up another job before quitting their current job, they should not feel that they must stay in a situation in which they are not happy. Loyalty and obligation are important, but like everything else, they must be held in balance. Most importantly, remember that no one is indispensable. Someone else will take your place and the organization will continue to operate. In fact, as a leader, it is your responsibility to make sure that the organization is not dependent on any one individual, including you.

As we ordered dessert (chocolate, of course, for grandpa), he said that he knew he had not yet given me any specific skills to help me in my new job. He said he would but, "I feel we need to talk about the whole context of leadership before we focus on the tools necessary to perform the job." The reason he felt that was so important was that many of these initial decisions would affect my whole career because patterns of behavior would start to be formed. Also, he had one other principle that he wanted me to understand before I accepted any other leadership positions in the future.

Grandpa does not believe that there are universal leaders. Rather, leaders are successful because they are the right person, with the right leadership style, in the right place at the right time. More gifted leaders can be successful in more places at more times, but even they will not always be successful if it is the wrong fit. He said we have numerous famous examples from military leaders, athletic coaches and even business CEOs in which the person was incredibly successful in one setting but could not be successful in another setting that was a bad fit.

> Don't become so enamored with your success that you think you can take any leadership job and be successful. Know who you are and know your style of leadership. Study the setting of the new job and try to determine if there will be a fit. If more people (both applicants and decision-makers) studied and thought about the fit, there would be more success-ful leaders and more leaders happy with their job. Remember, the fit helps determine success but fit will most certainly also determine the happiness of the leaders in the position.

The bill arrived, and after squabbling about who would pay, we agreed to split it evenly. I also knew that we had taken the discus-sion as far as we could for both of us for one day. When I originally sought out grandpa to help me get ready for my new job, I realized that I had many myths in my head and aspects of the job that I had not thought about. Most notably, I never thought about having to

set personal boundaries, about being happy in the job beyond being successful and the idea of no universal leaders (or even universal styles and skills of leadership). Our luncheon discussion gave
me so much "food for thought" that I needed to "digest" it before
moving on. So, we said goodbye and agreed to meet again next
week.

❖

3

The Trail Not Taken

(When You Choose a Trail, You Lose Options)

I was glad that we had gaps in time between these visits because I needed to reflect in order to understand what grandpa was telling me. I also realized after our lunch that some of these concepts applied to a much broader set of situations than just leadership positions. In particular, I started to think about how patterns of behavior, once established, tend to perpetuate themselves and define one's typical behavior. I can already see that in my teaching position in terms of student expectations, time spent preparing for class, amount of student graded materials and experimentation with new teaching strategies. Just like grandpa had said that a leadership job is never done, the same could be said of being a teacher. There is always more that can be done to improve student success; and when you don't put in that effort, you become a mediocre teacher at best. I realize now that I never thought about the issue of balance and boundaries as a teacher.

Now, grandpa is making me realize that this needs to be a conscious decision in any profession. Ever since I started graduate school, I have always been a zealot in every professional activity, throwing myself fully into the endeavor. I am not saying that is going to change, but grandpa is at least telling me that it should be a conscious choice. Work or excellence in professional performance may be one's highest priority and the balance and boundaries should be adjusted accordingly. It may also be true that family and personal relationships are the highest priority which will create different boundaries and a different balance. Obviously, both choices have different negative and positive consequences; therefore it needs to be a decision and not action by default. It is also a decision that needs to be revisited throughout one's professional career because our lives change and so do we.

Grandpa's comments about finding happiness within my professional life also struck a new chord with me. I have become so achievement oriented that I have chased success and positive reinforcement without any reflection on what makes me happy. If people are achievement oriented and they do something well, it generates praise, giving an immediate tendency to do more of it to garner more accolades. While success and praise are wonderful, and it would not happen if you were not good at it, being successful and accomplished is not necessarily the same as being happy. I realized that being successful and happy needs to be thought of independently because I have lived my life thinking that doing things well was the path to happiness. Now, grandpa is making me think about leadership positions and whether they would make me happy, but he has also caused me to pause and reflect about teaching.

During my first few years of teaching at the community college I regularly received inquiries from the university and the private sector about whether I "had gotten community college teaching out of my system" and would I now be interested in pursuing avenues that "would make better use of my talents". I now realize that those inquiries have become less frequent. Probably, people stopped calling because they have given up on changing my mind, but I also realize that the longer I am in my current setting, the less desirable I am to these other opportunities. That is why this continued reflection on what makes me happy is important. If I am not truly happy teaching at a community college, I will not sustain my high energy, commitment and time to my teaching. Would assuming more leadership positions along with my teaching make me happier? Should I stay at the community college even if it means that I will lose the other opportunities? All questions that need to be answered and revisited on an on-going basis. For now, because I have already committed to next year, I will at least pursue the idea of teaching and being department chair, but I will revisit this decision next winter.

Grandpa is picking his favorite locations for these discussions and our next one is set for our local native plant botanical garden. I know that we will spend part of the time walking the paths within the garden, but I already know where we will end up for the bulk of this week's discussion – the bench in the redwood grove. The enormous redwoods with their incredibly straight trunks and fern undergrowth have always fascinated grandpa.

> I am glad that you will be serving as a department chair, but I think there are a number of reasons why talented faculty do not move into administrative leadership jobs. Some of the obvious ones are that they don't like having to deal with all of the problems that will come their way, and the pay difference is frequently insignificant (often even a lower daily rate of pay). However, the one I feel is the most important, and the one I want you to be sure to think about, is that faculty members lose their autonomy when they assume these leadership positions.

He reminded me that, as a department chair, I would be reporting to the dean, who in turn reports to the vice president, who in turn reports to the president. As a tenured faculty member, I had virtually complete control over my classroom, and I had to admit that it was one of the attractions to teaching. Now, grandpa reminded me, as a department chair I would be in an organizational hierarchy, and I would frequently need to seek approval to do certain parts of my job. It would be very different from the environment of being able to make my own decisions about how I taught my courses. As a faculty member, I had to interact with the department chair as a "superior" but I had always perceived him as a colleague, not a supervisor. That will change to some degree as a department chair reporting to a dean, and it would certainly change if I ever became a dean. Grandpa wanted me to go into this "leadership ladder" with my eyes wide open about how my work environment would change and, in particular, to realize the loss in autonomy.

Frequently in leadership positions the "supervisor" (or "superior") is somewhat "normal," but not always. Grandpa reminded me that this person would also have an enormous impact on my ability to do the job. He said, "I have some wonderful experiences with people who served as my mentors, but I also worked for some very unusual people." For grandpa, he said the two most prevalent types of unusual leaders he worked for were the authoritarian and the creative. The authoritarian types wanted to be directive, seen as "in charge" and "all knowing," while operating in a strict hierarchy. The creative types didn't want to be bothered by daily operating problems and issues, but rather wanted to focus on new ideas and new ways of doing things. In both cases, the people were far more complex, but grandpa was not interested in gossiping about their oddities (although he teased me by saying there were some great stories that maybe someday he would share with me). Instead, he wanted to use them to show how to act as a subordinate.

First, he said, "Virtually all leaders want to be 'loved' by their followers, even the ones who privately express disdain for them. If leaders perceive that people have more affection for you than they do for them, it seems to make them feel insecure; therefore be prepared to either be the object of attack or undermined or in some way publicly diminished."

Eventually, grandpa said he came to realize that these were acts of jealousy or envy and really were disguised compliments of how he was performing. However, that didn't eliminate his desire for retaliation. It is probably best to simply avoid retaliation, but if it is necessary, it must be done with subtlety and humor. Usually, there is remorse and reconciliation from the leader which would not be possible if someone publicly retaliated. Also, if people rise above these attacks, it increases their power base from their followers because people respect the use of restraint, and the leader respects being allowed to repent. However, in all of these cases, it is important to privately confront leaders so that they know you were hurt by their actions and that what they did was unfair and untrue.

Second, to be a good subordinate to any leader, a person needs to know when to disobey (or at least delay) a directive to avoid actions taken by leaders in an emotional state or a fit of pique. In education, there are very few actions that require immediate attention. Therefore, when a leader directs you to do something that you feel is not right, at least delay taking action – especially if the directive was given at a time in which it could simply be an emotional response to a situation. In essence, there are times when it is necessary to protect leaders from themselves. Likewise, it is also sometimes better when the leader is extremely agitated to even avoid interaction. If avoidance can keep leaders from saying things that they will later regret, give them space first. However, if avoidance simply means that someone else will be the object of their comments, it is better to step in and intercept the leader.

Grandpa said, "The most important aspect of building your leadership skills through being a subordinate is to learn from every experience. Obviously the critical first step is to watch each supervisor and learn the skills you admire and learn the behaviors you want to reject. The same can be true from watching and evaluating the people who report to you." It is amazing how much people can learn vicariously without having to experience the pain from their failings and by appreciating the joy from other people's successes. In both cases, it is critical to understand what they did to create the result. Grandpa said, "I did not believe in good and bad luck as being the cause because I feel people create their own luck by their actions and behaviors." Grandpa also said that I needed to take advantage of the inevitable opportunities that will present themselves. All experiences add to your skill set so try to say "yes" whenever an opportunity presents itself.

However, beyond that we need to recognize that all leaders are human, which means there are always parts of their job that they don't like to do and/or don't do well. Leaders will inevitably appreciate a subordinate taking over those responsibilities as long as the person performs at a level that brings credit to them. You must seize those opportunities, perform at a level of excellence that brings recognition but be sure the recognition goes to the leader, not you.

"While at times it may frustrate you to see the leader receiving credit for your work, some leaders will give the recognition back to you," grandpa continued. "For those who do not, don't worry because it is amazing how perceptive people will be, and many will know who actually did the work. But even more important than recognition is that you are actually being given the chances to act as the leader within that narrow capacity and develop important leadership skills. These are skills that you will then be able to take to your next position."

Emergencies also present a unique opportunity to build a special type of leadership skill. Grandpa explained that while participative management was the only survivable long-term style of management for higher education today (a topic he said we would discuss at a later date), there were times when a leader needed to use an authoritarian style of management. Those times were in an emergency such as an earthquake, a bomb threat, a fire, civil unrest, etc. It was expected under these circumstances that the leader would change styles and take charge. "Not just expected," grandpa said, "it was the responsibility of the leader to direct people in an emergency." For many, this required a skill that they had never used or developed, so when these situations arose, it was important for people like me to appropriately step forward and also to learn how others respond. Beyond a successful outcome to the emergency, there is also a tremendous bond created among the participants as a result of surviving the emergency. It is a bond that will help in future normal circumstances and give people a broader perspective beyond mundane squabbling. Perspective is a wonderful asset to getting things done. Again, more than anything, grandpa wanted to emphasize how people learn leadership and develop leadership skills in every situation, which is why leadership experience is probably the best teacher.

I had brought a thermos of coffee to the botanical gardens because I knew that grandpa loved his coffee, and I doubted that we could buy any coffee inside the gardens. I must admit I also enjoy a cup of really good, strong coffee from high quality beans and made with quality water. Since it was cool inside the redwood grove, the warmth from the steaming coffee felt particularly good and it helped grandpa make the transition from teaching to personal reflection.

He said, "When I started as a department chair I wanted to dismiss the old ways of doing things and use more thoughtful, newer methods. However, with time, I came to appreciate some of the virtues of the old ways." For example, the old hiring practices tended to exclude certain populations from equal access to job openings which meant the hiring process had to change. Unfortunately, the new processes tended to hire "by the numbers" and depended exclusively on some type of point system. While the merit of this approach is obvious, it also created a number of hiring mistakes.

Grandpa said, "I became so focused on an applicant's pedigree and 'points' that I stopped learning about the applicant as an individual during the hiring process." Grandpa was not suggesting that we go back to asking illegal questions or allowing prejudice to infiltrate the selection process but rather that we understand applicants beyond their degrees, their experience and the "points" generated from their answers to standardized questions. He said that learning who people were as individuals was an important ingredient in the selection process that was thrown out when the system was changed. His point, once more, was not in the specific but rather in the recognition that even flawed processes have virtues that should be preserved within change.

His use of this example triggered grandpa's memory about a lesson he learned as a department chair. Throughout his career he always felt that no matter what position he occupied, hiring new people was among his most important decisions. He said, "when I first became a department chair I emphasized degrees (and the institution that awarded them), performance in graduate school, type of experience, etc. In essence, I focused on the technical knowledge and competence of the applicant. However, experience taught me that extremely competent technical people could be very poor teachers and it was very difficult to train them to be good teachers. Yet, when I hired great teachers, it was easy to give them any additional technical training that they needed."

He also came to learn how hard it was to find great teachers and how easy it was to find extremely technically competent people. As a result, he changed his focus by 180 degrees so that he went looking for great teachers to hire and only looked at technical competence as a secondary consideration. Since all of the jobs published minimum qualifications, virtually everyone who applied and met those qualifications was competent. For the rest of his career, grandpa never took great teachers for granted and he was always searching for them. Of course, if he could get it all, he was thrilled.

As we finished the coffee under the redwoods, I could tell that grandpa was winding down for the day. Before we left, he said that while it might seem odd to talk about this at the beginning of my leadership career, he thought it was important because it was a concept that he failed to recognize until near the end of his career. It is about the idea of leaving a college to seek a job elsewhere. Grandpa said, "I had been raised with a strong sense of loyalty to my employer and to a college in which I had poured my 'heart and soul'. However, I learned the hard way that there comes a time to leave."

Sometimes, leaving is necessary for a person's own growth and happiness because the institution will not continue to provide those growth opportunities. The situation can be caused when there are simply no opportunities available in the foreseeable future or caused by having reached a glass ceiling in the minds of the trustees ("it is hard to be a prophet in your own land"). Whatever the case, you might only be able to continue to grow and be happy by seeking a job at another college.

Grandpa said that even though he understood the situation, he felt such loyalty to his first college that he was reluctant to leave because he felt his presence helped the college even when it did not help him personally. The other situation is that sometimes it is also better for the organization for a person to leave. It is easy to become stale, and leaders should probably only stay in a position for less than 10 years (even as a vice president or president). An institution and a person gain comfort in longevity but at some point the institution can lose its creativity and start to be simply a maintenance effort. In grandpa's case, he had been involved in a controversial decision by the board in which the decision went against grandpa, even though he had the support of the people inside the college. He thought his presence would help to reduce the tension from the decision, but eventually he decided that his presence might actually be perpetuating the unrest. In any event, he said, "For all of these reasons I left, and I should have left sooner." What he wanted me to understand was the importance of keeping this option as an alternative but also to be vigilant about not staying too long in one job, even when people want you to stay. Once again, he reiterated what he had said at a previous time. "There is the right time at the right place for each leader and it is important to understand when a change would benefit everyone."

After we finished our discussion about leaving a college, we decided it was also time to leave the botanical garden. Once again grandpa gave me a lot to think about, but when I dropped him off at his house he said, "When we meet next week, we need to start talking about how to be an effective leader." He suggested going for a hike rather than just sitting. He said that his brain works better when the blood is circulating!

I started driving home but I was worried that I would forget what we had discussed today and that I needed to make some notes. So, I pulled over to the side of the road, retrieved my tablet from my backpack and made the following list.

Notes from The Botanical Garden Walk

1. Patterns of behavior, once established, tend to perpetuate themselves and define your typical behavior. They become unplanned habits.

2. A leadership job is never done, which means there is always the issue of balance and boundaries. All decisions involving balance and boundaries have costs associated with them, so this needs to be a conscious decision, not a decision by default to habits.

3. While success and praise are wonderful, and would not happen if you were not good at your job, being successful and accomplished in a leadership position is not necessarily the same as being happy.

4. Faculty members lose their autonomy when they assume leadership positions.

5. It is probably best to simply avoid retaliation against a supervisor or person of power, but if it is necessary, it must be done with subtlety. However, it is equally important to privately confront leaders so that they know you were hurt by their actions and that what they did was unfair or untrue. In addition, to be a good subordinate to any leader, a person needs to know when to disobey (or at least delay) a directive.

6. Watch each supervisor and learn the skills you admire and learn the behaviors you want to reject. The same can be true from watching and evaluating the people who report to you.

7. Take advantage of the inevitable opportunities that will present themselves. All experiences add to your skill set, so try to say "yes" whenever an opportunity presents itself. People learn leadership and develop leadership skills in every situation, which is why all leadership experience is a great teacher.

8. Hiring new people is among a leader's most important decisions.

9. A leader must develop multiple leadership styles so that the best style can be used in different situations.

10. Sometimes, leaving is necessary for a person's own growth and happiness because the institution will not continue to provide growth opportunities for them. Conversely, it is easy to become stale in your job so sometimes it is also better for the organization for a person to leave. Remember, there is the right time at the right place for each leader and it is important to understand when a change would benefit everyone.

4

"Follow the Yellow Brick Road"

After having three talks with grandpa, I was truly curious about his years at the college. I thought the best way to satisfy my interest was another visit to the college archives in the library before our next visit. While most of the information I found was fairly routine, I did come across a file that must have come from his office after he retired. In it, among other papers, was a handout that appeared to have been used in a speech or presentation that he made. The librarian made a copy of it for me, and I decided I would take it with me on our hike and ask grandpa about it.

I picked grandpa up at his house and we drove to the trailhead. The discussion in the car was just about the usual pleasantries, mostly updating grandpa on what mom and dad and my brother were doing. Of course, since we were in summer, it meant that we were in the middle of the baseball season and getting ready for football. So, a big part of our conversation focused on the prospects for grandma's teams (the Cubs and the Vikings) and grandpa's teams (the Dodgers, the Mariners and the Seahawks). Before we knew it, we had arrived at the trailhead; and I suddenly remembered this hike from when I was much younger. Grandpa said, "The hike we will be taking will be about five miles and the trail will wind mostly through the forest. I have always loved these forests with a collection of Douglas fir, western red cedar, western and mountain hemlock, big leaf maple and red alder with a full ground covering of sword ferns." It was a sunny day, but with so many tall trees the sunlight was filtered and it was wonderfully cool on the trail.

After we had walked for about 30 minutes we arrived at a small stream which provided a logical stopping point for a drink of water. Up to now we had both been enjoying the forest and mostly walking in silence except to make enough noise so that we did not surprise any large, wild creatures. Now that we had stopped, I brought out my find in the archives and showed it to grandpa. He laughed and said, "I vividly remember this speech. It was a speech on visionary leadership that I gave at a statewide meeting of the community college chief academic officers." Grandpa said, "Maybe this is as good of a place as any for us to start talking about more specific skills of being a leader." He went on to say, "Most of these skills apply to any leadership position but you should recognize that some of them may seem more applicable to positions higher in the 'food chain'." That seemed like an appropriate descriptor because we thought we had just heard a bear and decided to start walking again.

Once we started walking on the trail again (it really wasn't a bear), grandpa agreed to try to use the handout I found in the archives to recreate the speech for me. He said,

> As I recall, I started that speech by telling the audience that as I collected a number of ideas about being a visionary leader, I realized that 'visionary' is a term that is tossed around all the time and that people use it in many different ways. So, I thought that I probably ought to start by being clear on the

definition of a visionary. Webster's Dictionary said, "A visionary is one who purportedly experiences a vision or apparition connected to the supernatural. The visionary state is achieved via meditation, drugs, or lucid dreams. One example is St. Bernadette (who had a vision of and communed with the Blessed Virgin)." I said I am not sure that I can measure up to this calling. Of course, I was just kidding and that was certainly not Webster's preferred definition. However, there is an element to being a visionary leader in which, at times, the leader must be able to think "outside the box" or at least have ideas that are one to two standard deviations from the norm, but probably not as extreme as St. Bernadette!

Actually, when I thought about my suggestions for how to be a visionary leader, I came up with a list of ideas. But I reflected on those self-help books that I had read (e.g. the list of 100 ideas in *"Don't Sweat the Small Stuff"*) and I realized that all of the ideas sounded good when I read them, but within 48 hours I had forgotten to integrate them into my life. In fact, I even forgot the list itself, and my life was back to what it had always been. So, I knew for my audience, a simple list would not work. Instead people need a picture or a movie to play in their brain to remember my ideas. For these ideas to have any meaning to someone, the individual must internalize them.

I then tried to decide what T.V. show or movie I could use as an appropriate analogy. I used the Ozzie and Harriet television show once before in a speech, but although Harriet had many virtues, I don't think we would consider her a visionary. Then I thought about "Dr. Strangelove" but that vision was too bizarre (and more related to a few people I have worked with during my career). Of course I stayed away from all of Fellini's films.

Instead, I thought I would turn to the "Wizard of Oz" because everything someone needs to know about being a visionary leader was taught to us in the movie, "Wizard of Oz". Of course, if you are not familiar with the movie, it would be helpful to watch it or at least look at segments on the internet. First, the leader is sometimes the Wizard – not the fictional one, but the guy behind the curtain. A person frequently has to orchestrate the leadership of the college in a clandestine manner from behind the curtain. And, like the "professor" behind the curtain, a person needs to create the vision and that vision, of course, is the Emerald City. As in real life, a leader has to play more than one role. On the journey to achieve the vision, the leader has to change roles from the professor and become Dorothy. We have many candidates for the other characters in the quest to achieve the vision. The community is, of course, represented by the munchkins. The leader will certainly confront characters within the college who do not have the courage to try something new and different, the brains to understand what one is trying to accomplish for the college or the heart to be motivated by anything other than self-interest. Hopefully, one works in a good place where your supervisor is represented by the Good Witch of the

North, but, unfortunately, I know some people have to work with the Wicked Witch of the West.

When I think about being a visionary, I am not talking about just coming up with a vision statement – which is usually more like a slogan. Being a visionary means the leader has laid out a path for the future (the yellow brick road) that will help reach the desired destination. The people within the span of leadership (Dorothy, the Tin Man, the Scarecrow and the Lion) need to work together and agree on the destination – the Emerald City of Oz. The vision needs to be simple enough that everyone understands and knows what they have to do to get there – ideally this is where everyone sings the song "Follow the Yellow Brick Road". It needs to be complex enough to be a real path – the yellow brick road wound through numerous adventures, just as a college does. Finally, the vision needs to be creative enough so the destination merits the effort – and its accomplishment creates something greater than just a collection of individual achievements -- the vision of Oz!

As much as I enjoyed the metaphor, I didn't want to beat it to death but I hope it gave the audience a mental framework to understand the visionary quest. On the more practical side, I needed to use the Wizard of Oz metaphor to explain how the leader accomplishes the job. To that end, I had a series of observations as to what creates a successful visionary, which I outlined on the handout you found. And, I might add, the system desperately needs more visionary leaders at every level!

THE WIZARD OF OZ
VISIONARY LEADERSHIP TIPS

1. Learn to be a good and authentic listener (A heart for the Tin Man – genuine caring about the thoughts, feelings and beliefs of others).

2. Ignore or at least challenge conventional wisdom. (A brain for the Scarecrow – think through the consequences and restrictions on your own).

3. Don't fear failure. Be willing to take risks (Courage for the Lion – plain and simple).

4. Set aside time to work on the big ideas (Creating Oz).

5. You can never be satisfied with the status quo. (This isn't Kansas anymore.)

6. For any specific change, determine the largest organizational unit capable of making the change and focus on it for the easiest solution (Water on the Wicked Witch of the West).

7. Communicate frequently, accurately and in a transparent manner ("Follow the Yellow Brick Road").

8. Take pride and satisfaction in the quality of the effort. (They made it to Oz even though it was an illusion.)

9. Build as many named partnerships as possible. (Dorothy, the Lion, the Scarecrow and the Tin Man were a partnership).

10. The first order of business is to instill hope and optimism among employees (What Dorothy did for the "team").

Grandpa went on to say, "I guess if I am going to try to remember everything else that I said, you'd better let me see the handout." So, I gave grandpa the handout.

I said to grandpa, "If you don't mind, could you just start at the top of your handout and work our way through it?" Grandpa agreed and said that being a good and authentic listener is like the Tin Man having a heart because it begins with genuinely caring about other people and what they have to say. It is not about trying to fool the speaker and only pretending to listen. There are many techniques to being a good listener (maintain eye contact, don't be thinking of other things while trying to listen, take notes, repeat to the speaker what one heard, look for elements in which the listener can provide positive feedback, etc.), but if the listener has the heart of the Tin Man and really cares about what the speaker has to say, all of these techniques will come naturally. Ironically, these techniques are most critical when the listener is trying to focus on the comments of the speaker but would really rather be doing and thinking about other things. That is, the techniques are critical when someone is only pretending to listen. However, even authentic listeners should not ignore the techniques because they are part of the skill set necessary to actually hear what is being said.

The other important part of being an authentic listener is that leaders not only care about speakers who support their position or give compliments, but listen to everyone. At times, it means leaders must use third parties (surveys, focus groups, third party interviews) because people will have difficulty saying critical messages to the leader directly. Also, when listening, a person should try not to be defensive. Sometimes, people will make comments that are based on their perceptions which the leader knows are incorrect. While leaders want to provide them with accurate information, don't dismiss their perception. Perception is reality to the perceiver. If other people have that same perception, it may be critical for the leader to take some broader action to remedy the misperception. As a result, the speaker is giving important negative information, and the leader needs the speaker's help in understanding the source of the misperception.

On a much more positive side, being an authentic listener will go a long way to creating a climate in which ideas are welcomed and sought. People within the organization will bring ideas to leaders if they believe that leaders will really listen to them. Since new ideas are a critical component of a visionary leader's quiver, a leader must work to create a climate that fosters ideas. One of the most important lessons that needs to be learned by visionary leaders is that they do not need to be the originator of all new ideas. Rather, the leader needs to cultivate those ideas in others, listen when they are presented and facilitate the implementation of those ideas that will benefit students and the organization. This includes the concept that leaders should not engage others with predetermined solutions to situations but rather that they remain open to looking at alternatives.

Being an authentic listener is the art of creating a place in which people feel the leader tries to say "yes," rather than "no" so that people are able to overcome the feeling of vulnerability that is associated with advocating a new idea to the leader. No one wants to feel foolish, especially in the eyes of the leader. That is why it is critical to listen to the idea being presented with genuine interest and try to at least extract elements that you can support. But, in all cases, the person has to feel appreciated for presenting the idea, even when the leader must reject it in its entirety. That person's next idea may be a great one. Also remember, probably everyone has at least one great idea and the leader wants to hear it.

Moving down the list, grandpa said that every leader needs to be like the Scarecrow and use the brain that he or she was given. This concept is particularly critical to the visionary leader in terms of being well grounded and having a complete understanding of constraints to implementing new ideas. Institutions, particularly colleges, seem to relish the status quo and have a built-in inertia to resist new ideas. Frequently the processes themselves for introducing change are so elaborate that they provide resistance to change without even presenting an opposition. Grandpa did not think that was an accident. One of the ironies of higher education is that it is supposed to be a bastion of intellectual pursuit of new ideas. Yet when it comes to the actual institution itself, those same people are often very resistant to any change in the college.

Besides overcoming processes that resist change, visionary leaders are frequently told that their idea cannot be implemented because it violates some rule, regulation or law. It turns out that most people within the organization have never read the rules, regulations or laws, but even if they had, it was a long time ago and not in the context of the proposed new idea. It seems that most versions of these restrictions are really a form of oral history that has been passed among colleagues and among generations of colleagues. Unfortunately, it is often either incomplete or actually wrong. That is why visionary leaders needs to be like the Scarecrow and use their brain by reading the rules, regulations and laws themselves. Frequently, one finds an opening in the restrictions (or possible alternative interpretations) when they are read carefully by the leader. Too many good ideas have not been pursued because the person was told that the idea violated a rule, restriction or a law. Read it yourself, and even if the rules or laws restrict implementation, the visionary leader may see an opportunity to amend, change or remove the restriction. Remember, there is no formal restriction that cannot be changed.

Grandpa went on to say that a visionary leader needs courage. At some level we are all like the Cowardly Lion and need the courage to take risks. Everyone wants to always be successful and never fail. However, the critical threshold is when the fear of failure keeps the leader from implementing new ideas. Creativity is just an interesting pastime if the ideas are not implemented. Of course, if leaders don't implement any new ideas, they cannot fail. New ideas are not safe or guaranteed, so they do involve risk; but unless leaders are risk takers, they cannot be visionaries. For perfectionists, it is the fear of failure that paralyzes them; but for most people it is the fear, or simply the dislike, of being criticized or being made to feel stupid for taking the risk or having to deal with the conflict of change.

While no one likes criticism, the critic (or opponent) must usually be placed in context. Legitimate critics usually don't criticize but instead either try to figure out how to make the idea successful or determine why it failed, so that everyone can learn from the experience. However, they usually don't attack, place blame or ridicule a reasoned decision. For many of the other critics, there is usually an alternative motivation. Many people oppose new ideas even before they are implemented because they mean more work for the people in opposition, although the reasons given for opposition are never that transparent. Other people oppose a new idea because they bolster their position with their constituents from opposition and conflict. The power base for these individuals is based on conflict, and, in the absence of conflict, they lose their power and their leadership role. Whatever the context, the visionary leader needs to anticipate opposition to new ideas and criticism if ideas fail. That is why it takes courage to push forward.

It is also the reason why a visionary leader must create a safe environment for others. The goal is not just to be a visionary leader but a visionary institution. That means others need to be able to take risks and also implement new ideas. If they do take the risk and they are successful, be sure they receive the credit. If they are unsuccessful, and the leader probably approved the action, the leader should step forward and take the blame for having approved it. When people know that the leader has "their back," they will be much more willing to try other ventures in the future.

Even failure needs a context. There are many good ideas that fail for reasons other than the quality of the idea. Sometimes it is simply the wrong time or the wrong place for the idea. Sometimes it is the way the idea was implemented, not the idea itself. Process for implementation matters, and, if done improperly, it can cause opposition that is aimed at the idea but is really based on the process, not the idea. That is why successful ideas often occurred in the second or third place they are tried and not the first. It is also why the visionary leader is always looking for the ideas of others – even when they failed. Grandpa finished his comments on courage by saying that he never liked failure or criticism but he loved the thrill of the chase – the thrill of trying to do something new and different. The thrill of the chase is probably a common element among visionary leaders.

Of course, grandpa went on to say, it is pretty hard to be a visionary leader without a vision!

> That was really what I was after in the next point on the handout. You have to create Oz which was a vision in its entirety and for us it particularly means creating the vision of the Emerald City. As I said before, when I talk about a vision, I am not talking about a slogan but instead it is a clear concept of the future as the leader would define it. The problem is that for most of us mortals, that vision does not just come to us as an epiphany (or a dream after being hit on the head). It requires a great deal of thought, reflection and in some cases research to develop a vision. That is not going to happen if you do not set aside time to work on the big ideas. At times, that big idea may be an important social issue that is only a tangent to the vision but it is still a critical focus of the leader. Ideally, a vision would embrace this social

issue but even if it doesn't, if you took the time, you might develop a strategy for making some progress on the issue, and that is important.

The dilemma for the leader is that daily operational issues (including personnel issues) can be all consuming. There is probably not enough available time to spend as much energy as a leader would like to on all of these operational issues. So at the end of every day, a person could always spend more time and make it better.

Besides the price you pay in your personal life by not setting a boundary, leaders also pay a price in their professional performance by not setting a boundary on time spent on operational issues. Leaders need to schedule and plan for time to be spent on the big issues as they relate to their leadership unit (whether it is a department, a division or a college). First and foremost, leaders should be thinking about how their area of responsibility can be distinctive and superior from all other comparable areas. This is the critical component of the vision. Second, leaders should be thinking about how they will solve the major problems and issues facing their leadership (financial, personnel, process, etc.). Third, take the time to dream about how you could radically change things to improve the situation for students. Finally, take the time to think about major social issues in which higher education needs to play a role in developing the solutions. These big issue thoughts will not be a single reflection but an on-going process that you work on continually. The reason that all of this reflection is important is because it helps the leader to spread the widest net possible and to always be looking for ways to make progress. In the case of the dream and the social issues, you are not looking for full implementation in one action but rather the chance to implement slices of your ideas. In the case of the other two parts of the vision, the work you have done should be integrated into the vision that is articulated to your followers. However, don't lose sight of the critical element which is that none of this will happen unless the leaders set aside time to work on the big issues and they don't allow daily operational issues to consume them.

As we walked toward the vista on the trail, grandpa said,

If you spend any time thinking about the big issues, you soon realize the next point which says that you can never be satisfied with the status quo (this isn't Kansas anymore). If leaders are satisfied with the current state, then they would have no thoughts on the big issues and it would mean that they think everything is perfect. Obviously, perfect never happens but it can be a delusion of excellence. When an entity achieves its objectives and is publicly recognized for its excellence, it can cause some people to want to rest on their laurels. Unfortunately, as you remain static, everyone else is changing, progressing and improving so simple maintenance of today's excellence becomes tomorrow's mediocrity. We all know that technology has shown us that if we don't change, we first become obsolete and eventually we can become irrelevant. However, it would be a mistake to think that this is restricted to technology. It really is just the most obvious product of the status quo, but it is equally true in all other elements of leadership responsibility.

Grandpa did not think that anyone wanted to be obsolete, mediocre or irrelevant so it was important to understand why leaders would be satisfied with the status quo. Simply put, grandpa felt it was the path of least resistance. There is usually enormous resistance to change or doing anything different from the way it has been done in the past, especially if it was successful. Probably the more time that has passed without change, the greater the resistance to change. In some cases, it is simply a resistance to the work required to change (particularly among some people near the end of their career). In other cases, it is a genuine discomfort or actual fear of change that causes the resistance. And, the resistance can be both overt as well as passive-aggressive. At a later time grandpa and I would talk about dealing with this resistance, but for now grandpa just wanted me to understand the temptation for a leader to be satisfied with the status quo because it would be a much easier path of leadership. Grandpa also wanted to remind me about the group reaction to change. If it is successful, a number of people who resisted it will claim that they were always a supporter and if it fails, people will point to you as the cause. That takes us back to the idea that a visionary leader must be a risk taker.

As we arrived at the vista, grandpa said he was now old and when it comes to hiking he is not a risk taker! That meant he wanted to rest. Frankly, I wanted to rest as well, but I also knew he was partially kidding because I knew the vista was the destination of our hike. While we sat on a log enjoying the panoramic view, drinking the water that each of us had brought and sharing my trail mix (with dark chocolate chips of course), it gave me a chance to respond to everything grandpa had told me so far. I said that I understood everything he had discussed and that it all made sense to me but I didn't know how I would ever remember all of

it. Grandpa said that when we returned, we could add some notes
to the handout beyond the ones I had already written because the
handout was just an outline and he had expected his audience to
add their own notes during the speech.

> But more importantly, just remember the Wizard of
> Oz and it should trigger your recall. Based on what
> we have discussed so far, it is easy to remember the
> heart of the Tin Man, the brain of the Scarecrow,
> the courage of the Lion, the vision of Oz and it is not
> Kansas anymore. If you can recall those parts of the
> film, you will probably remember the most impor-
> tant parts of what we discussed, and it is the reason
> I tried to use that metaphor. The hard part will not
> be the recall of our discussion; the challenge will
> be to incorporate it into your everyday leadership
> performance so that you are not even conscious of
> practicing visionary leadership. Unfortunately, there
> is no quick solution. It simply requires performing as
> many leadership functions as possible while trying
> to be mindful of the qualities for being a visionary
> leader.

As we started back to the car, I knew we still had over two miles
to hike but at least more of it would be downhill. I hoped the same
would be true of learning the other five elements described on
the handout. Grandpa said the sixth element was really about effectively implementing change.

> Always look for the easiest solution, which is why I de-
> scribed it as pouring water on the Wicked Witch of
> the West. That was much easier than trying to fight
> her and the flying monkeys and the same needs to

be true of implementing change. Find the largest organizational unit capable of making the change and focus on it. This is the idea of not trying to be heroic or politically correct or democratic in implementing change. Find the places in the organization that support the change and narrow it down to the ones with the most capable leaders who can successfully implement and manage the change.

When you create successful pockets of change, it will spread. It spreads in part because some of the fears of resistance have been shown to be unfounded. In other cases, people will see the benefits of the change and will not want to be left out. The strategy is really a different application of the old maxim that "success breeds success". When the change is outside of the existing organizational units, develop a "team" that will work together to simultaneously implement the different elements of the plan. Speed of implementation can be an asset so that a leader does not have to continually fight resistance. Just get on with it and deal with the resistance all at one time. If the change is successful, the resistance will evaporate. If it is not, accept responsibility, reverse your action and acknowledge your mistake. Then move on to the next idea.

One other thought that grandpa shared with me was that, when a person is looking for change leaders, don't just pick the usual candidates.

More than anything, you need someone who has a passion for the change and has strong interpersonal skills. Sometimes that person is a current leader but a person should not simply be assigned to a leadership position who doesn't share the passion for the change. I often had success recruiting unexpected leaders by approaching retirees, people on leave who wanted part-time work, people looking for a change in their life, etc. The important characteristics were the passion and the skills, not the institutional pedigree. However, it can be helpful if the passion can be paired with the pedigree to gain institutional credibility.

Grandpa laughed when he saw the next listing on the handout.

I guess I am practicing what I preached when I said you need to communicate frequently, accurately and in a transparent manner – at least I hope that is what I am doing with you. The song, "Follow the Yellow Brick Road" communicated over and over to the participants about how they would reach the vision of Oz, but, of course, your situations will be more complicated. That is why it is so important for the visionary leader to continually be a teacher. Usually great leaders are excellent teachers (although the opposite is not necessarily true). The leader should not approach a situation with the idea of having to "sell" the vision or the route to the vision. Rather, it is a teaching situation in which the leader explains the rationale for the vision and the path so that others adopt both of them out of their own reasoning from the available information. When people adopt the vision themselves out of their own reasoning it is a much more powerful motivator and creates a much stronger bond with the leader. The goal for the leader is to get everyone to that point, but it is important to remember that faculty, administrators and staff are just like your students in that they all learn differently. As a result, in teaching about the vision, just like in a classroom, the leader needs to appeal to all of the different learning styles – especially in terms of using both data and narrative.

In trying to explain the vision, also try to avoid win/lose or right/wrong positions. If this is honest communication, leaders want to hear all forms of commentary, not just the ones that agree with them, because it is possible that the vision and the path can be improved. The ideas need to be presented in a way that explains how you arrived at your positions but opens it up to a dialog that would improve it. Remember, different positions are usually just different perceptions attached to the same set of data and observations. This idea of openness is why the communication must be transparent. Also, if the leader is completely transparent, with no hidden agendas or "errors of omission," it will build another bond of trust and allow the ideas to grow into better ideas.

For the first time, grandpa said how much he was enjoying our talks and interacting as professionals, instead of just talking as relatives. He said it has even been enhanced by where we have the talks because he is also enjoying sharing some of his favorite places with me. This provided the perfect segue to his next point. The visionary leader needs to take pride and satisfaction in the quality of the effort – the journey. Dorothy, the Tin Man, the Scarecrow and the Lion made it to Oz even though it was an illusion. Moreover, even if the journey had not given each of them what they wanted, one believes that they were glad for having the experience and the satisfaction of working together, and it was not just dependent on the outcome.

Current political and pedagogical doctrine is extremely focused on defined outcomes as the measure of success while discounting the effort. It is understood that these beliefs were driven by years of inappropriately only measuring effort, independent of outcomes, especially in terms of student performance. However, for the visionary leader it is a different set of circumstances. As mentioned earlier, the visionary leader is a risk taker so some ideas will be blocked prior to implementation and others will not be successful. Yet, the effort has merit unto itself. The leader who is blocked will have learned what changes must be made for future endeavors to avoid a similar problem. In addition, a person always dissects failures to learn from them. Furthermore, if people were only measured by their successes, they would take far fewer risks, only focus on simple changes and have far fewer significant changes.

> Remember that personal responsibility has limits to the variables within your control. Success and failure are often determined by variables beyond your control. If you want to be a visionary leader, enjoy the successes (and the praise that will come from them) but also appreciate exceptional effort for ideas that are blocked or failed. And, that is even more important in terms of supporting people who work for you when they try to develop and implement new ideas.

We were over half way back to the car and the trailhead, but we both decided it was a good time to stop, take a rest and have some water. On our way up the trail we had seen an old abandoned windmill which was rusted and obviously not in working order. It stood as a monument to earlier times. The windmill reminded grandpa of earlier times and digging wells. A time when people worked in a much more cooperative way and realized that sometimes working together benefited all parties more than was possible from working independently. While grandpa, by his own admission, was a highly competitive person who loved to win (I remembered this from family card games), he also mourned the lack of cooperation among colleagues. "At times," he said, "it almost felt as if people would rather fail than ask for help because somehow it was perceived that asking for help was a sign of weakness. I felt that this 'going it alone' attitude had also caused too many people to avoid using partnerships with colleagues in other colleges and with organizations outside the college."

Grandpa's attitude about partnerships was the opposite. He felt that a visionary leader tries to build as many named partnerships as possible. Going back to the Wizard of Oz metaphor, he said it was the partnership that was developed among Dorothy, the Tin Man, the Scarecrow and the Lion that helped them reach the Emerald City. The same is true in a college. Partnerships allow a leader to combine expertise, energy and most important, resources. In the case of the college forming partnerships with outside agencies, it frequently means that it is at no cost to the college because the other partners bring the resources. These partnerships work and remain viable as long as the partnership provides mutual benefits to all parties. It is important to remember that one of the things that a college has to offer to a partner is public relations value, charitable donation value, and help in acquiring foundation or government agency support. The college needs to remember that one of the benefits that it derives from a partnership with prestigious partners (e.g. major universities) is implied endorsement.

It was now time to walk the final leg of the hike. Grandpa said he needed a few minutes to stretch out his stiff muscles (he no longer does these hikes on a regular basis). When he was ready to go, we started off and grandpa had a gleam in his eye as he started to talk about the last item on the handout. He said he had saved the best for last – the item that he felt was most important to being a visionary leader. The first order of business for visionary leaders is to instill trust, hope and optimism among their followers. Certainly Dorothy did that for her partners on the journey in Oz.

Visionary leaders often become so caught up in generating new ideas or solutions to problems that they forget about process and morale. No matter how bad the situation is, people will work tirelessly on improving the situation if they have hope that things will be better and if they trust their leader. Everybody wants their situation to improve, but they are not willing to invest their time, energy and expertise if they think the situation is hopeless or if they don't trust the leader and the direction being provided by the leader. This is the critical starting point when hard times have been experienced, but it is equally applicable when the prior experience has been one of success. Visionary leaders may have great ideas, but if they want followers, they need to first instill trust and second a sense of hope and optimism in the future under their leadership. This is such a simple concept but it is the critical one. If you reflect on people you believed were great leaders, they all created within their followers a sense of optimism about the future and they wanted to help the group, college or country move toward the future they foresaw.

We made it back to the car. I could tell that grandpa was physically exhausted from the hike, and I was mentally exhausted from all of the information he had given to me. I knew that my first order of business was to go home and add as many notes as I could remember to the handout. I had scribbled notes on the handout as we hiked but I knew that if I didn't decode them quickly, I would not remember what my notes meant. We mostly rode in silence on the way home – grandpa was talked out and I was trying to mentally add to my notes. I dropped grandpa off at his house and we agreed to meet again next week. He said, "I will call to give you the details of our next meeting location and to answer any questions you have in trying to decipher your notes." I drove home from grandpa's place with a sense of a wonderful new bond with him. I was still his granddaughter and I cherished that relationship. However, today I was also his colleague and that felt very special.

❖

5

Hiking Awards: The Leadership Oscars

G randpa called and said, "For our conversation this week, I want to do something completely different. Could you come by around 11:30 and pick me up? We will swing by the Fantasy Café and Market to pick up lunch. I hope you don't mind but I ordered the same for both of us. I chose my favorite sandwich which is a turkey pesto Panini with caramelized onions, fresh spinach and Havarti cheese. I added to our sandwich order a premium bottle of root beer and chocolate chip cookies for each of us. After we pick up lunch, I will show you where to drive."

We went to the café and picked up our lunches which were waiting for us. Grandpa insisted on paying because he said I was doing all the driving. He then directed me on a 30-minute drive which ended at a state park that was a former artillery fort in the early 1900s. It was a beautiful combination of forests, seaside cliffs and even the remains of old artillery batteries. Grandpa said, "I cannot think of a better place for an old man to talk about his past, especially when accompanied by tasty food and an appreciative audience." After parking the car, we walked with our food to a picnic table near the top of one of the bluffs that gave us a panoramic view of the water, the edge of the forest and even a glimpse of one of the artillery batteries.

Today, more so than the other days, grandpa was taking the initiative.

> The last time you brought a handout from one of my old speeches that you found in the archives. This time I brought a handout from another speech I wrote after I retired but never delivered, so you will not find any remnants of it in the college archives. However, before I share that with you, I want to talk a little bit about when I was growing up – believe it or not, it is relevant. When I was young we did not own a television, nor did any of our neighbors. We listened on the radio to programs like the Lone Ranger or sporting events like the Brooklyn Dodgers. We also spent a lot of time reading books (for me mostly mysteries like the Hardy Boys).

> With the passage of time, we became knowledgeable about television; and one day our parents brought one home. My father installed the antenna and we became enchanted with the black and white pictures. Eventually, the available television programs expanded to three national stations and, because we were living in a large city, we also had four local stations. In the beginning, the programs didn't matter because the whole experience seemed magical, but with the passage of time and the increased offering, we became more discriminating viewers. Around this same time, on Saturdays, I would also go with my best friend on our bikes to see movies. It was a great adventure too because we were out all day on our own, and the movie was an integral part of our escapade. Beyond these experiences as a child, it is

also important to mention that, like you, I grew up and worked my entire career in the middle of the television and film industry. Why am I telling you all of this background? I wanted you to know that movies and television shows have always held an important place in my fantasy life. And, for me, even later in life, those same television shows and movies (plus some newer ones) have provided powerful associations with different types of behavior. So it is only logical that when I reflect on my leadership career, I would think in terms of famous television shows and movies.

Beyond my continual fascination with these various forms of entertainment, I also continued to believe after the "Wizard of Oz" speech that talking about leadership required some form of image association as I had done in that presentation. Around that same time I was being asked to make other presentations on leadership, so I tried to develop another form of visualization or image association using another movie and other leadership traits beyond being a visionary leader. Unfortunately, I could not find another individual movie that worked as well so I came up with a slightly different approach that I wanted to share with you today.

I crafted what I called my "Leadership Top Ten List – The Oscar and Emmy Awards of Leadership" in which I associated a series of critical leadership traits with 10 of my all-time favorite movies and television shows. As I talk about leadership, the movie and television metaphors work for me because there is always one that personifies the characteristics I am describing, and it is so much easier to remember the leadership traits through these associations. While I consider most of these choices to be classics, I also realize that virtually all of them were shown before you were born. I encourage you to go watch the movies and at least a couple of episodes of the television shows. It is easy to do. Just search under the title and view them on You Tube or go to www.imdb.com and search on the title. If you do, my associations will make more sense to you. Actually, I am afraid if you don't watch them and understand their character portrayals, this exercise will be lost on you. So, I guess I am saying you have a homework assignment to watch these classic movies and television shows, but I will pay for the popcorn!

In any event, I am also going to give you some brief descriptive capsules for each of them so that, until you watch them, you can still understand my associations between the traits and the movie or television show. Nevertheless, this is also the reason that I never delivered the speech. I still talked about leadership traits but I never used this handout or this technique because I always feared that my audience, like you, would not be familiar with the movies or the television shows (and I could not make them go home and watch them). I was afraid that the whole idea of the associations would not work if they were not familiar with them. I even tried to find more current shows and movies but nothing seemed to fit. Now, the internet has come to my rescue. Between You

Tube and www.imdb.com, you can easily see clips or complete episodes from all of them.

Before we go any farther on our walk, I want to be sure this is what you would like to do on our walk today. I am afraid it will be like last week where I am essentially giving you a leadership lecture while we walk.

I explained to grandpa that this was precisely what I had in mind when I first came to talk with him. It would not bother me if our walk was in the form of a lecture if he didn't mind that I would occasionally need to stop to write notes. Having reassured grandpa that he was doing what I wanted, he gave me the handout he would have used in the speech.

The Leadership Top Ten List
The Oscar and Emmy Awards of Leadership

1. 12 Angry Men
   a. Leadership is about using your influence, not the authority associated with your position.

2. One Flew Over the Cuckoo's Nest
   a. ½ of 1% of any group cause the problems – students, faculty, community.

3. Music Man
   a. Leadership traits need to be internalized so that you are using genuine beliefs and feelings.

4. Mr. Holland's Opus
   a. No act of kindness goes unappreciated.
   b. Put in the time and work hard.

5. It's a Wonderful Life
   a. Leaders have the responsibility to create a community among the people they are leading.
   b. Earn the respect of others through demonstrating honesty, integrity, thoughtfulness and intelligence.

6. M*A*S*H
   a. Try to keep your ego separate from your job.
   b. Avoid making yourself the center of attention.
   c. Be action oriented.

7. Carol Burnett Show
   a. Great leaders surround themselves with great people – hopefully better than you.
   b. Transparency breeds trust.
   c. Be a caring person and show your grace.

8. Gunsmoke
   a. Know which "hills you are willing to die on".

9. Sanford and Son
   a. If you are going to hire people to help, be sure you show them what to do and how you want it done.
   b. Make sure the people who work for you know that you care about them.

10. Colombo
    a. Whenever possible, try to greet people with a smile.
    b. Continually seek advice and suggestions.
    c. "A patient response is always better than a quick reaction."
    d. Assume positive intent in the actions of others until they prove you wrong.

12 ANGRY MEN

A jury of 12 men has just heard a murder trial and has begun its deliberations on the guilt or innocence of the accused. When the jurors begin the deliberations, the jurors openly discuss how this is an "open and shut case" in which the defendant is clearly guilty. The jury polls its members and 11 members vote for guilty but Juror Number 8 does not. The movie is then the portrayal of the dynamics among the 12 men in which Juror Number 8 slowly converts all 12 of the men to a not guilty verdict. Stars Henry Fonda with a great supporting cast that included many well-known actors.

Leadership Trait: Leadership is about using your influence, not the authority associated with your position.

The lesson learned from Juror Number 8 is that leadership comes from influencing others by your reasoning, your preparation, your knowledge, your presentation, and your character, instead of directing others through the authority of your position. It is easier and less time consuming to simply use your authority, make a decision and tell your followers what is going to happen. However, it is much more powerful if you guide them to a conclusion in which you share the outcome. They may even improve the outcome through their involvement. But in any event, they will be far more enthusiastic about supporting a decision they helped to develop or at least a decision that they independently arrived at and therefore independently agree with the leader. This is really the cornerstone of participative management, and there are entire books written about how to do it and why it is a superior form of management for most situa tions (but not all).

Beyond the superiority of the leadership technique, I wanted to talk about why it is important in understanding leadership and strengthening leadership positions. Most people think that the authority of their position is a given power associated with the position. However, true authority is really bestowed on leaders by their followers. Look at most revolutions and you will see entrenched leaders acting within their legal limits but they are also operating outside of what their followers consider their legitimate authority. Accordingly, the followers believe that the leaders have abused their authority and need to be removed. In the more modest cases, like work environments, the more leaders use their authority (or power) to make decisions, the less authority (or power) is given to them by their followers. Given enough erosion, followers will have low morale, a lack of support for change, sabotage and eventually make efforts to remove the leader. The opposite is also true. The more a leader moves people to decisions that they support, the more power they bestow on the leader. Juror Number 8 had no designated authority but as the deliberations continued, he clearly became the leader of the jury.

When you are successful, you then need to resist the opposite problem. Don't exploit your power to your own advantage. The pendulum can swing too far and people will tend to give successful leaders too much power. The most visible exploitation of that success is to garner undeserved benefits. Not only does that create a moral dilemma, but it also can cause the pendulum to swing back in the other direction.

Grandpa's last piece of advice on using the power of the position had to do with circumstances in which, as the leader, you have to make decisions that are not unanimous.

> When it comes down to it, do what you think is right. Don't make decisions to be popular or political or to advance your career if you think they are wrong or not fair or are morally corrupt. Not only will those decisions haunt you, but there is nothing worse than having those decisions create problems for you when you didn't want to do it that way in the first place. If you do what you know is right, you can live with the consequences. As a leader, you don't just act out of personal self-interest, and as a leader of an organization, you must make sure that the organization doesn't always just act out of the organization's self-interest. There are long-term social and societal measures that need to be attended to beyond short-term measures that provide immediate reinforcement. Again, going back to 12 Angry Men, Juror Number 8 was simply doing what he thought was right in our judicial system in which the accused must be found guilty beyond a reasonable doubt.

ONE FLEW OVER THE CUCKOO'S NEST

Randal Patrick McMurphy, a prison inmate, decides that he could get out of work details by pretending to be mentally disturbed and by being sent to a mental institution. He successfully convinces prison authorities and is sent to an institution where they also believe he is mentally ill. He immediately rebels against the rules and organizes the inmates to challenge them. His adversary is the lead nurse, Nurse Ratched, who is more like a prison guard or a dictator than a nurse. In the end, the institution decides that he is beyond control and they administer a frontal lobotomy. Stars Jack Nicholson and Louise Fletcher. Based on the book by Ken Kesey.

Leadership Trait: ½ of 1% of any group cause the problems – students, faculty, community

Grandpa said that the purpose of including the movie, "One Flew Over the Cuckoo's Nest", was to discuss the importance of maintaining perspective while in a leadership position. The relevant message of the movie is that McMurphy initially went to the mental institution as a gimmick without being honestly diagnosed as having a mental or emotional disorder. But, in the eyes of the institution (and in turn the eyes of society) and maybe even eventually in his own eyes, he was declared as having a disorder requiring him to remain in the institution. As a result, both he and society lost all perspective as to the real McMurphy. It is critical as a leader that we don't lose that perspective and forget who we really are.

When I was a college president, I would always say there was a ½ of 1% rule in which at least ½ of 1% of every group had emotionally unbalanced people within the group. So, if the college had 1,000 employees (administrators, faculty, staff – both full-time and part-time), then I could expect that I would have to deal with at least 5 unbalanced people at any given time. Of course, if you then realize that the college had nearly 20,000 students every semester, you are talking about 100 unbalanced people. And then, the ultimate extrapolation was the community!

It was important to remember that ½ of 1% because you did not want them to represent the other 99 ½ % of the group and you did not want them to consume you. In the case of the former, these distressed people could say really unpleasant things, and you needed to avoid taking their comments personally. That is a very hard lesson to learn and one I struggled with constantly. In the case of the latter, it was important to recognize how time consuming it was to deal with this population and to take measures to contain their use of your time. However, most important of all was to maintain perspective by actively interacting with the other 99 ½ %. That means, for example, that you need to leave your office and interact with others. Even within the 99 ½ % there are a significant number of people who are completely negative about everything and want to complain or enjoy conflict. If you are passive, you will only see a negative world because people, by and large, only come to see you when they are upset, have a problem or want to argue. The majority of people are happy, productive and supportive, but they will not come to you to tell you. However, if you go to them, you can hear the positive side of your followers.

As a leader, part of your job is to visit the asylum but don't stay there. In the movie there is a character named the "Chief" who, in the end, escapes to Canada. Be sure you maintain your perspective and go home after the visit. You don't want to become the McMurphy of leadership.

THE MUSIC MAN

"Professor" Harold Hill is a professional con man who decides to leave the train in River City, Iowa with the intent of performing his usual scam. He will convince the residents of River City that they need to form a boys' band and that, for a price, he will arrange the acquisition of instruments and uniforms, along with training each boy to play his selected instrument. Of course, it is his intent to simply collect the money and skip town. Harold Hill's plan is disrupted by his falling in love with Marian, the librarian. As a result, he cannot bring himself to execute the con so he orders the uniforms and the instruments and trains the boys to play in the band. Written by Meredith Wilson and starring Robert Preston and Shirley Jones.

Leadership Trait: Leadership traits need to be internalized so that you are using genuine beliefs and feelings.

When I asked about "The Music Man," grandpa said,

I included it because too many people in leadership positions are not genuine. That is, people perform the job the way they feel others want them to act and/or on the basis of how they feel a leader should act; but in both cases, they are exhibiting traits that they do not genuinely possess or even believe in. When it occurs in its most manipulative form, leaders are like Professor Harold Hill and are just trying to con their constituents. However, unlike the music man, they do not get to leave town quickly (nor fall in love with the librarian) so eventually their "true colors" show.

In some ways this creates even more resentment among followers because they may not like the leadership style of the real person and now they also don't trust him or her. People in leadership roles cannot fake their leadership style and traits for extended periods of time. Eventually, a person's true characteristics will betray them. I think it is so important to internalize the desired traits and avoid pretending to be someone that you are not. If you believe in yourself and you believe that a particular leadership style or trait is the correct one for the situation, then be honest with your performance and, if necessary, justify it. Be authentic. It will garner far more respect from your followers than to later be discovered as a fraud.

The same circumstances apply when seeking a leadership position. Remember, there is no right style (or traits) for every situation at every point in time. The key to success is to match your genuine leadership characteristics to a situation that is appropriate and desirous of those characteristics. If you fake it, down the road both you and everyone else will be unhappy. Of course, the worst case is that you were not selected for a position because you guessed wrong – what they really wanted was someone like your genuine self, not your false portrayal!

As a general rule, higher education, especially among the faculty, demands a leader with a participative management style for policy development and general operating decisions (obviously they don't want that style during an emergency). Since this is a widely held belief, it is the portrayal of believing in participative management that is the most frequently faked leadership trait. Unfortunately, there are many leaders who embrace an authoritarian style of leadership but try to feign support for participative decision making. In the end, this almost always results in disintegration of the relationship between followers and leaders because the participation is really a charade. It also usually results in anger on the part of the followers because they feel they were duped and that they wasted both their time and energy. Participative management only works in the long run if the leader genuinely embraces and believes in its principles.

Before we leave "The Music Man," grandpa wanted to mention another problem that occasionally happens when people try to adopt a leadership style that is not genuine. In a few rare instances, people watched the wrong movie and have the wrong image they are following. This is particularly true when people assume leadership positions for the first time. For example, instead of watching "Mr. Smith Goes to Washington", they watched "Patton". So even though it does not reflect who they really are, they become extremely authoritarian because that is their view of a strong leader. Again, it is the problem of not allowing your leadership to be a natural extension of your personality and personal characteristics.

MR. HOLLAND'S OPUS

A moderately successful musician, Glenn Holland, decides that he would like to change his life so that he has more time to spend with his wife and to work on writing one great piece of music. He decides that the way to accomplish this is to become a high school music teacher. Mr. Holland discovers that the demands of teaching are much greater than he had anticipated and he faces numerous challenges in his role as a teacher – both with the dynamics of the high school in terms of other faculty and the administration along with the difficulties in teaching students about music. Added to this frustration is the discovery that his son is deaf and he has no idea how to relate his love of music to his son. The result is that Mr. Holland does not have the free time that he desires, and it takes him nearly 30 years to write his piece of music, his opus. Now that it is finally written, he cannot find the financial backing to have it performed.

After working as a teacher for 30 years, Mr. Holland is informed that the high school music program is being discontinued and that he will no longer have a teaching position. On his final day, he is escorted to the auditorium where many of his former students have gathered to perform as an orchestra. He is called to the podium and he conducts the inaugural performance of his opus to the applause of a packed auditorium of admiring Mr. Holland supporters. Starring Richard Dreyfuss.

Leadership Traits: No act of kindness goes unappreciated. Put in the time and work hard.

Grandpa selected "Mr. Holland's Opus" to represent two different perspectives – the perspective of the leadership skills it represents but also the perspective of being a leader in higher education.

As a leader, it is important to possess the virtues of any good employee and model that behavior for everyone in the organization. Do not think of yourself as being above the standards and requirements of everyone else. That behavior begins with working hard and putting in the hours. People will notice if even from afar. They notice when the lights are on in your office and they notice when your car is in the parking lot. If you work hard, it encourages everyone else to work a little harder.

Grandpa had not really thought that people noticed this type of thing until he had been a president for a couple of years. He realized they were watching when a few employees approached him because they were concerned about how much time he was spending on the job; they were worried that he was burning himself out.

In a similar vein, leaders should not feel that certain jobs are beneath them and expect others to do the work for them. This can be as simple as picking up trash on campus, fixing the coffee in the morning, or changing a light bulb. Again, it is important to remember that people notice everything you do. I had people tell me that if the president can pick up trash then they could too. Also, there is a woman who, to this day, remembers seeing me fix a light in her building. The important point is that people are watching and noticing what you do. In some cases, it motivates them to act in a like manner and in other situations, it simply helps them to feel more connected to you.

Because the actions of the leader are exaggerated in their impact, it is also important to remember that these actions extend to how you greet people, remembering people's names and all acts of kindness. Usually we do all of these acts as just an extrapolation of our personality and assume that we are just doing what everyone else does. We also assume that, as a result, no one gives any particular notice to these actions. However, just as Mr. Holland discovered on that last day in the auditorium, people do care and they do notice. No act of kindness by a leader goes unnoticed. All leaders ought to do this as simply being decent human beings, but in the context of this list, I wanted you to know that it matters. Furthermore, as you might guess, all of the negative actions are equally noticed with the corresponding negative effects on people.

Grandpa also had one other leadership trait that he felt was important to associate with this movie that we talked about with visionary leaders during last week's discussion, but is worth repeating. Exceptional leaders need to be excellent teachers. In particular, they need to be able to communicate effectively so that everyone understands their vision and the reason for their actions. Also, they need to be able to explain financial conditions, laws and external variables because that understanding of these complex issues is critical to people knowing the context of the leadership you are trying to provide. Mr. Holland, in the end, will be remembered because of his teaching ability, not his musical skills.

Besides the message of this movie regarding leadership skills, grandpa also felt that the movie had some important messages for those involved in leadership positions in higher education. Great teaching is often taken for granted. Everyone thinks that because they went to school they are experts in education and can teach. Some people, like Mr. Holland, go into the profession thinking that it will be easy and will give them free time. Those individuals usually teach that way and destine themselves to mediocrity. Others realize what it will take to do the job the right way and soon learn they will have even less free time. Maybe, if they work at it, they will be a great teacher, but great teachers are a true rarity. Any leader in higher education needs to recognize that reality and treasure great teaching.

It is much easier to give a great teacher additional technical background than it is to train a subject expert on how to be a great teacher. Unfortunately, not enough academic leaders realize this fact. As a result, academic pedigrees and awards are recognized while many great teachers toil in anonymity. Even among the great teachers, those who are flamboyant or extremely popular with students are noticed while the others change lives without being appropriately appreciated by their leaders. Again, a lesson taught by Mr. Holland.

Finally, grandpa said, "Mr. Holland's Opus has one more lesson for us. When budgets are tight, the core mission of academic institutions becomes redefined." Inevitably, the first programs attacked are the fine arts, vocational education and physical education (or athletic teams that don't generate a profit). While this is not the place for this dialog, it raises an interesting commentary about our value system and also fails to support a population of students who are primarily connected to education through athletics or fine arts or specific vocational disciplines. The core mission needs to be defined outside the context of financial crisis and once defined needs to be sustained, through some means, in the face of the inevitable periodic budget crisis. Once gone, it will be difficult to resuscitate an eliminated program, like Mr. Holland's music program.

IT'S A WONDERFUL LIFE

George Bailey lives a life that he "inherited" as opposed to the life he had planned. He marries his high school sweetheart and has four children but he ends up spending his life perpetuating the Bailey Building and Loan which he inherited from his father instead of going to college and seeing the world. This business works to genuinely help the people of Bedford Falls and to hold the evil town developer, Mr. Potter, at bay. The business survives on a shoestring but comes crashing down when George's Uncle Bailey loses the bank deposit. George decides that everyone would be better off if he were dead, so he sets out to commit suicide.

George is saved from his suicide attempt by his guardian angel, Clarence. Clarence not only saves him but grants his wish by showing him what life would have been like if he had never lived. Seeing what a difference he made, George is granted his desire to return to the world as he knows it. When he returns home, he discovers that all of the townspeople and all of his friends have raised the necessary money to save the Building and Loan. Directed by Frank Capra and starring Jimmy Stewart and Donna Reed.

Leadership Traits: Leaders have the responsibility to create a community among the people they are leading. Earn the respect of others through demonstrating honesty, integrity, thoughtfulness and intelligence.

In some ways, grandpa said, "'It's A Wonderful Life' embraces all of the personal leadership characteristics that we are talking about today." However, because he thought that some of the other associations were stronger, he wanted to use this movie to focus on two critical attributes of a successful leader. George Bailey was a beloved and respected leader in Bedford Falls, yet he never intended to assume that role and didn't even realize how people felt about him. He was a leader by default. This is actually a case of being a genuine leader without any real position of authority. It happened by the way George Bailey conducted his life and his business. In both situations, he acted with honesty, integrity, thoughtfulness and intelligence. Of course, in his work with the building and loan, his exhibited behavior affected people's lives. Nevertheless, he was not doing it because he read that it was what leaders should do or because it was the keystone to good customer service. He simply did it because that was how he thought people should lead their lives. When those virtues are demonstrated in a genuine manner, it creates respect among the people you are trying to lead even though you are not doing it for that reason.

An organization cannot realize its full potential unless leaders can create a community among the people they are leading. The whole organization is greater than the sum of the parts. It is the sense of community which creates the work environment and the culture of the organization.

In a college, great teachers can individually create exceptional learning inside their classrooms, but the learning experience for students can be much greater if it encompasses more than just the classroom experience. Is this a place where faculty want to be involved in the college outside of the classroom? Are all employees engaged with the institution beyond their minimum job requirements? Is this an enjoyable place to be and, as a result, everyone looks forward to going to work and spending time there? Do the people of the organization care about the well-being of each other? When an organization can have this vibrant sense of community, the organization as a whole and the individuals within it will create something greater than just the individual faculty-student classroom interaction learning experience. The movie dramatically exposes this concept when it shows George Bailey the contrast in the community if he had not been a part of it. Pottersville (as the town would have been called) is nowhere near the quality of the town of Bedford Falls which evolved under the leadership of George Bailey. It is the difference in the whole created by a skilled leader.

M*A*S*H

M*A*S*H (mobile army surgical hospital) was both a very successful movie and a long-running television show that was based on the movie. The setting for both of these is South Korea during the Korean War. While the shows are about all members of the army unit, the focus is on the surgeons (including the commanding officer) and the head nurse. The movie and the television shows were a collection of episodes that dealt with the realities of war but showed how highly competent medical professionals needed to use humor and practical jokes to mentally cope with the horrific realities of war that they faced on a daily basis. The movie starred Elliot Gould, Donald Sutherland and Sally Kellerman. The television series was a true ensemble cast but the leads throughout the life of the series were Alan Alda and Loretta Swit. It is believed that the final episode of M*A*S*H was the most watched episode in television history.

Leadership Traits: Try to keep your ego separate from your job. Avoid making yourself the center of attention. Be action oriented.

M*A*S*H was one of my favorite television shows because of the cast that had been assembled (and even changed over time) for the show. It was a wonderful ensemble of actors and the scripts were well written. However, beyond the entertainment value, M*A*S*H demonstrated the qualities of a leadership team as it faced some of the most difficult situations imaginable as a surgical hospital in a war zone. The M*A*S*H team always understood their mission and never allowed personal aggrandizement to take precedence over fulfilling the mission. Even when the one character in the cast would occasionally slip, he was mercilessly harassed for letting his ego get in the way of his job. The mission of the unit was always protected and given first priority. Leaders must always drive the organization to make fulfillment of the organization's mission the priority and the foundation for all decisions. In the case of a college, it means that the priority and focus needs to be on students and the successful fulfillment of student educational goals. That does not necessarily mean that it is done at the expense of the well-being of college employees, but the opposite cannot be true. Students cannot be expendable to enhance employee benefits and desires.

Like the medical personnel in M*A*S*H, it also means that individual ego needs to be kept separate from the job. And, that mantra is most important for the leader. Performing the role of the leader is not to promote the reputation and image of the leader. Therefore, those activities which are done for the purpose of achieving that goal are inappropriate. The leader needs to stay focused on driving the organization to fulfill its mission and not be engaged in self-promotion. It also means that when organization dialog is occurring, leaders need to keep the focus of the dialog on the issues and not make themselves the center of attention. If leaders can maintain this separation of job and ego (or identity), besides the obvious benefit to the organization, it will provide the leader with a measure of insulation against unwarranted criticism and personal attacks.

The final lesson from M*A*S*H is to remember that the leader needs to be action oriented. In higher education, where participative management has such a high priority, it is easy to fall into the trap of talking issues to death and failing to act. However, it also does not mean that the leader arbitrarily or prematurely cuts off discussion and becomes an authoritarian leader. Rather, from the outset, the leader establishes the necessary parameters to insure that a decision is made and implemented in a timely manner. Organizations can live with time constraints on participation as long as they are known up front and are not used as a manipulative tool. While higher education does not generally have the "life and death" issues of a M*A*S*H unit, it is still important to follow their example of acting in a timely way so that the organization makes expeditious progress toward the fulfillment of the mission and does not wallow in indecisiveness. It is particularly true when facing a problem. The faster a problem can be solved, the better. If it is allowed to fester, it can create ancillary problems making the situation even more difficult to solve.

Grandpa said, "An old man can only sit at a picnic table so long before rigor mortis sets in! I am afraid we are getting close to that time. Maybe that is enough for today and we should do the second half of the list next week. In the meantime, don't forget to do your internet searches of these movies and shows."

With my agreement, because my head was already swimming with everything he had told me, we gathered our belongings and walked back to my car. I took grandpa home with the promise of picking him up next week at the same time for our discussion of the second half of the list.

6

Climbing Awards: The Leadership Emmys

When I picked grandpa up, he said, "Since we started this list last week in the state park, I think we should go back there this week to finish it." This time, grandpa brought a small cooler because he said he wanted to have something special for our lunch dessert. He had us drive to an old general store where we picked up sandwiches (tuna salad on pumpernickel for me and chicken salad on sour dough for grandpa), chips and soft drinks. However, on the way out, I discovered the need for the cooler because grandpa wanted to buy ice cream. I ordered a cup of chocolate decadence (three types of chocolate) and he ordered his favorite – black licorice ice cream. With the ice cream in the cooler and the rest of our food in a tote bag, we set off for the state park. This time I even knew how to find my way.

As we pulled into the parking lot, grandpa said, "I wanted to come back to the park but I wanted you to see it from a different perspective." This time we hiked down a path to the beach and walked until we came to a set of large logs that had washed ashore in a way that provided a place to set out food and give us a back rest while we ate. All the while, as we sat eating our lunch, we could watch the ocean. Now, I know why grandpa likes to come here so often.

After enjoying our lunch (and especially the ice cream), grandpa said, "Assuming you can stand another leadership lecture, it is time to get to work." And once again he brought out his "Leadership Top Ten List". Since I was rested from last week and very contented from our food and our location, I reassured grandpa that I was excited about tackling number seven.

THE CAROL BURNETT SHOW

The Carol Burnett Show was a weekly television show that was on the air for 11 years with 278 episodes. During the life of the show it won 25 prime time Emmy Awards. It was billed as a variety show, and every week a guest artist joined the cast. However, the show is best remembered for its comedy sketches which included the rest of the ensemble – Harvey Korman, Tim Conway and Vicki Lawrence. The format and structure of certain sketches were repeated with the cast playing the same characters but placed in different situations. The guest artist (even when not a comedian) was usually included with some role in selected sketches.

Leadership Traits: Great leaders surround themselves with great people – hopefully better than you. Transparency breeds trust. Be a caring person and show your grace.

I was a regular viewer of the show; and Carol Burnett, as the clear star of the show, did an exceptional job of demonstrating a critical principle of leadership in the way she assembled and managed the performance of her cast members. The principle personified by Carol Burnett is that great leaders work to surround themselves with great people. That begins by putting your ego in check and trying to get people around you who are even better than you. While that principle seems logical and easy, too many leaders surround themselves with people who are weaker than they are out of the hope that it will make them look better by comparison. That might even be true but the overall performance of the leader and the organization will suffer.

Of course, it is not enough to just select the right people. The leader also needs to be sure that all of them are serving in the proper role to maximize their talents. And even then, the job is not done unless the leader empowers them. This is frequently where the leadership process falls apart. The leader selects good people, puts them in the proper role but does not empower them. In particular, often out of insecurity, the leader holds on to all of the control. Not only will this make the organization less functional, but it will be very unfulfilling for the subordinates. If the leader has truly attracted quality people, under these circumstances, they will not stay.

As shown in the writings of Jim Collins in *"Good to Great,"* he calls this concept "getting the right people on the bus". However, don't forget the other two steps of getting them in the right seats on the bus and empowering them to perform their job in a way that maximizes the organization's utilization of their talents. Carol Burnett demonstrated this concept in an effective way by the fact that she assembled people around her in the cast who were probably even better comedians than her. But she did not stop there.

The scripts were written in a manner that allowed all cast members to share equally in the comedic punch lines. They all got the laughs. It wasn't just a case of the cast members setting up the situation for Carol to receive the laugh. She surrounded herself with the right people, in the right roles and she empowered them.

Grandpa said there were also more recent comedy sitcoms which demonstrated these leadership traits. Most notable is "Seinfeld". In "Seinfeld", Jerry Seinfeld surrounded himself with strong comedic actors to play the roles of George, Elaine, Kramer and Newman while letting them share equally in the comedic punch lines. Grandpa went on to say,

I thought I would be remiss if I left our discussion of the Carol Burnett Show without talking about another characteristic of how the show was managed. Carol also exemplified the demonstration of transparency. The show was always taped before a live audience. She did not edit out all of the mistakes or the times when the cast would ad lib and break up the other cast members. By being so transparent and honest, the audience became endeared to her. In fact, most people would agree that the most memorable moments of the show were the unscripted moments. The same lesson needs to be learned by leaders. Transparency and honesty cultivates endearment and trust. In a transparent environment, even mistakes that are openly visible can make the leader seem more human. When that happens, the followers feel closer to their leaders and are more willing to trust them and follow them.

Carol Burnett always acted as a genuine, caring person who allowed her emotional response to situations guide her actions. This was particularly evident in her portion of the show where she allowed the audience to ask her unscripted questions. While most of the questions were funny, there were occasionally more touching questions in which she answered in a very caring and gracious manner. Again, this transparency, along with a sense of caring and grace towards members of the audience, allowed her fans to be attracted to her.

The same is true for a leader. Sometimes, people confuse a demonstration of caring and grace with weakness in a leader. They could not be more wrong. Leaders can be strong and capable of making the tough decisions while at the same time being caring and gracious individuals. If they do combine these attributes, people are much more willing to follow their leadership.

By the way, grandpa added, "This technique of allowing the audience to ask any question they wish, is another form of transparency in which leaders can demonstrate the full breadth of their attributes (from humor to intellect, from personal to policy issues) and the audience will feel they know you better after the session even if there are only a few questions."

GUNSMOKE

Gunsmoke was a television series that was on primetime television for 20 years. While there is a debate about whether it was the longest running primetime television series, it did have the most scripted episodes at 635. It was a western drama in which the star was the sheriff of Dodge City, Kansas. Each week he faced the necessity to resolve some problem related to fulfilling his duties as sheriff. While there were a number of supporting cast members, the scripts focused on the actions of the sheriff, Matt Dillon (as played by James Arness).

Leadership Traits: Know which "hills you are willing to die on".

Grandpa smiled when he started to talk about "Gunsmoke". He reminisced about this time period being the era of television and movie western dramas. He said he chose "Gunsmoke" because he watched it regularly, but he also said that he could just as easily used other television westerns (like "Bonanza" or "Maverick") or western movies as examples; but he specifically wanted to focus on the character of Sheriff Matt Dillon to talk about this leadership characteristic. Specifically, leaders need to know which "hills they are willing to die on".

> A leader faces so many potential battles and conflicts that it is not possible to take all of them to their ultimate conclusion – even when you always think you are in the right. At the same time, you need to clearly understand which principles are not negotiable.

> Matt Dillon exemplified this behavior (particularly in contrast to other westerns at the time) because he always used judgment over a gunfight. He tried to

solve problems without resorting to violence but had a clear line where he would not back up or negotiate. Besides knowing which "hills he was willing to die on," he also demonstrated that his first preference was to negotiate a solution so that the possibility of dying was not even an option. The same is true of a leader. In every situation, try to find a solution without letting it deteriorate into a conflict with opposing sides. In essence, avoid the gunfight.

Grandpa said it was hard sometimes when the actions of a person were offensive or obnoxious, but he always tried to keep the idea of finding a mutually agreeable solution as the highest priority. He also knew which "fights" he would not take to the ultimate conclusion. By the way, grandpa said, "Once you know which 'hills you are willing to die on', it is best to keep that list yourself!"

SANFORD AND SON

Sanford and Son was a television sitcom about a 65 year-old man (Fred Sanford) who runs a junk yard with his 30-something year-old son (Lamont). Fred is a long-time widower who is always looking for "get rich quick" schemes. Mostly the sitcom focuses on the relationship between Fred and his son with occasional interactions with Fred's other family members (e.g. his sister-in-law Esther) or friends (e.g. Grady). The show starred Redd Foxx and Demond Wilson.

Leadership Traits: If you are going to hire people to help, be sure you show them what to do and how you want it done. Make sure the people who work for you know that you care about them.

You might think this was my oddest choice of a television show or movie to demonstrate leadership skills. Fred Sanford was a cantankerous old man who was always ridiculing Lamont. Lamont always talked about his father being an "old fool". In all of their actions, they were probably the antithesis of good leadership. However, there are two traits that they demonstrated which do merit being recognized.

Grandpa said, "It shows that even in situations like Sanford and Son, there are leadership lessons to be learned."

First and foremost, through all of the banter, it was clear that Fred and Lamont genuinely loved each other, and they allowed it to be periodically shown so that each was reassured as to the feelings of the other party. The same needs to be true for a leader. The people who work for you need to know that you care about them as professionals and as individuals. Sometimes, we become so caught up in the work that we forget to let the people around us know that we care about them. As you might guess, people will perform better for someone who cares about them than they will for someone who simply sees them as a means to an end.

Second, in a very strange way, the interactions between Fred and Lamont demonstrated another leadership trait. Both of them were explicit about how they wanted the other person to act in their respective roles in running the business. While a junk yard is probably not the model organization we are looking for and the nature of their interactions are not the manner we desire, the content of their communication is the outcome a leader desires. Too often, leaders do not specifically explain to the people who work for them what they want them to do and how they want them to do it. When leaders fail to do that, they are usually operating on the assumption that the person should know how to do the job without being told. However, anyone who has worked in different organizations for different leaders knows how different the expectations can be for someone doing the same job. That is why explicit direction is important and can avoid future misunderstandings.

COLOMBO

"Colombo" was a detective story starring a homicide lieutenant (Lieutenant Colombo) in the Los Angeles Police Department. Unlike most television detective stories, the beginning of the episode showed the commission of the murder and revealed the identity of the murderer. The show then followed Lieutenant Colombo's investigation and the suspense was in how he would solve the murder and trip up the guilty parties. He always drove an old, somewhat dilapidated car and he always wore a wrinkled trench coat. The show became famous for the lieutenant's questioning of the suspect; and after he appeared to be finished and was walking away, he would say, "just one more thing" while he asked the critical question. The show starred Peter Falk.

Leadership Traits: Whenever possible, try to greet people with a smile. Continually seek advice and suggestions. "A patient response is always better than a quick reaction."Assume positive intent in the actions of others until they prove you wrong.

"Columbo" was one of my favorite television shows and certainly my favorite detective show because it was a show about solving problems and puzzles by a man who was always calm, smart and self-effacing. A leader frequently has to face difficult problems and puzzles and Lieutenant Columbo personifies a wonderful way to approach these situations. He was always polite and concerned about all people involved in the crime, even in his interactions with the suspected murderer. Leaders need to adopt those same manners when confronting a problem. It will usually help to diffuse a situation if the leader is calm, polite and self-effacing even though other people may be out of control. In fact, as a general rule, it is always helpful for a leader to interact with all people in this manner and even better if in normal situations it can be done with a smile.

Grandpa said, "When I walked around campus, I always tried to smile as I greeted people because it was genuine and showed everyone that I was glad to be there. It also mirrored my optimism about whatever challenge the college was facing."

The method used by Columbo also teaches us about how to approach problems. In every situation, Columbo was not quick to react and instead took a deliberative approach to develop a patient response. The same needs to be true of a leader. One needs to be decisive so the leader cannot take too long to respond; but at the same time the leader needs to take enough time to have a thoughtful response. There will never be enough time to gather all information and have a perfect solution, so this is a balancing act of taking enough time to have sufficient information and reflection while still delivering a timely decision. Finally, in arriving at the decision, the leader needs to be willing to seek advice, input and suggestions from all relevant parties. Sometimes leaders think that asking for advice is a sign of weakness, but it is really a sign of strength to be able to solicit a wide array of input, maintain control of the situation and develop a decision that utilizes the best advice available.

Grandpa said that this completed our quick walk through his "Leadership Top Ten List" but he worried that it would lose some of its meaning to me because I was too young to remember (or ever know) the movie and television show references. I promised that between the internet searches, You Tube, cable television and Netflix, I would find the movies and samples of the television shows so that I could have the pictures in my mind that he wanted to have represented for these various leadership traits. I also knew that my "Wizard of Oz" handout on the wall of my office would soon have a companion, "The Oscar and Emmy Awards of Leadership" handout, which would help me to incorporate everything grandpa talked to me about over these last few weeks.

As we gathered the trash from our lunch, grandpa said, "There is still more that could be discussed but I think we have gone far enough for now. We have covered numerous aspects of leadership and it should give you a good start on your leadership career. I think the biggest challenge you will face is deciding what parts of our discussions you want to use and how to use them. I still feel that integrating these concepts into your leadership is very hard and can only come from experience. I will be interested to see how that unfolds as your career progresses and you accept more leadership situations. In the immediate future, I know you will be a great department chair."

Grandpa finished by telling me that grandma and he were thinking of moving and that he was glad that we had the chance to spend so much time together before that happened. However, he said, "No matter where I am living, you can always call me or come see me."

HIKING TO THE SUMMIT

7

Walking the Talk

I t has now been nearly 15 years since grandpa and I had our walks through leadership. Fortunately, his wisdom has helped me and I have been able to have a successful climb up the administrative ladder. Following my work as department chair, I was selected as our division dean and most recently, I have been serving as the executive vice president for academic affairs and student services. Last month I learned that I have been chosen to be the president of a nearby college and I will start the job in two months.

When grandpa and I started our walks, he had only been retired for a few years. In the year following those walks, just as he had told me, grandpa and grandma moved to a home that is nearly 1200 miles away. It has meant that we see each other at holidays and family gatherings but, between my work schedules and the distance, we have not been able to spend time together discussing leadership as we did that summer on our walks. And somehow, emails and phone conversations have not been a satisfactory replacement.

I am confident about starting my new job, but I also have some anxiety about assuming the presidency. Perhaps, even more importantly, I really like my grandparents and I miss spending time with them. So, I have arranged for them to spend a few weeks with me before I start my new job, and grandpa has agreed to resume our walks through leadership.

Our first "walk" was really just getting a cup of coffee and sitting in a local park overlooking the water. Even though grandpa may not walk as fast or as far as we did in our first set of walks, he is still capable of short hikes. We went to the park because I was eager to start our discussions, and I wanted to fill him in on some of my experiences during the intervening years.

Grandpa, over the last 15 years, I have tried to remember everything you told me on our walks and I even occasionally reread my notes, but I always have had two pieces of paper either on my desk or stuck to the wall – "The Wizard of Oz Visionary Leadership Tips" and "The Oscar and Emmy Awards of Leadership." Those ideas have been important for me, but I have also found that it is much easier to use some of the ideas more than others. Maybe that's why my career over the last 15 years has been a mixture of successes and challenges or failures. I like to think that the successes far outnumber the failures, but I seem to remember the failures much more vividly. It is also what I have missed about being so far apart. I have been unable to discuss my challenges with you and to share my successes. In thinking about today, I made notes about specific circumstances that have occurred over my years in administration because I want to talk to you about them. In the cases of the successes, I want to share them with you so that you can see that your ideas worked. For the challenges, I want to know what you would have done differently because I think these situations could reoccur in my new job.

I did not spend a lot of time trying to organize these situations but I have tried to group them to correspond to the two lists. Just as you did on our walks, I would like to start with the "Wizard of Oz" list. Your first point referred to the importance of being a good and authentic listener. I have been able to do that when people approach me with personal problems and on "low stakes" issues. However, when I am trying to garner support for a big issue, I seem to exclusively focus on winning my point of view. When opponents are talking, I sometimes stop listening because I am just trying to compose my rebuttal or next argument. At times, it has meant that the discussion has deteriorated into an argument and stood in the way of gaining consensus. Grandpa, how can I learn to be an authentic listener in all situations?

To begin with, don't be too hard on yourself – no one is an authentic listener all the time. It is the hardest when you are convinced you are right and a specific approach is the necessary path of action. Also, a critical part of your success is the energy you derive from wanting to always win in competitive situations. I always tried to fight these same urges by two messages I kept playing in my head. First, these are not competitions; they are problem-solving situations. So, rather than trying to be a winner or wanting everyone to know that the solution was your idea, you are trying to help others to arrive at the same solution on their own. It's even better, if they think it was their idea and they feel that you did not direct them to the solution (even if you were the one who showed them the logic of that outcome).

Second, remember the goal. You're trying to find the best solution for the problem with the broadest basis of consensus possible without sacrificing the quality of the solution. In the end, in these leadership roles, you will be evaluated by how well the institution solves its problems, not by who is credited with being the source of the solution. You need to set your ego aside in the short run (by not taking credit for the solution) because you will be rewarded in the long run as being the leader of a great college.

Ironically, in some of the most successful consensus building activities, many people feel they were the originators of the solution. Let them feel that pride in the outcome because, if it fails, be prepared for people to attribute the idea to you.

I still think it won't be easy to always be a good listener but I will try to focus more on the broader purpose and solution.

Of course, grandpa, in many cases your ideas worked great and were the reason that I was successful. One of those that worked so well was your suggestion to challenge conventional wisdom. Our college wanted to create a new academic calendar in which we reduced the number of days in a semester but increased the meeting time of the class sessions so that we kept the same amount of contact time between the students and their teachers. I was told by everyone at the college and all of my colleagues that the state education code and the state administrative regulations would not permit the college to make the changes that I wanted to make. So, taking your advice to challenge this conventional wisdom, I found all of the relevant sections within these laws and regulations, and I read all of them for myself. Through a very precise interpretation of these rules, I found a way for us to create the calendar we wanted. Conventional wisdom was wrong; and if I had listened to it, the compressed calendar would never have happened.

The loophole that I discovered was somewhat unique to our college; so to insure against being penalized for my interpretation, I had the state general counsel approve it for me before we implemented the new calendar. Even that was not easy for him because, by granting the approval, he was also "bucking" the state's conventional wisdom. Eventually, because the calendar was so successful, the state changed its laws and regulations so that all colleges in the state could participate in this new form of academic calendar. Nevertheless, the catalyst for this change was your belief that we should not just accept other people's beliefs and interpretations without reading the rules ourselves. This whole calendar situation was also consistent with your idea of trying to get to "yes". As a college, we first determined what calendar would be best, and I told everyone to not be constrained in their thinking by believing what people told us we could not do. I wanted people to first determine what we should do and I would figure out how to make it happen. And, that is exactly what happened.

> I am thrilled to hear that these ideas had a tangible benefit to you. And, I am particularly proud of you for not letting the system control your thinking and for finding a better way to educate students. Unfortunately, it seems as if too many leaders are easily discouraged from these kinds of roadblocks or simply don't want to make the effort that is required for "blazing a new trail". Maybe your efforts will encourage others to follow suit. But, even if it doesn't, I know this success will mean that you will always be willing to challenge conventional wisdom.

As I thought about situations over the last 15 years, I realized that, like the calendar, many situations related to many of your ideas and they could not be categorized into just one of the items on the list. When we originally talked about these ideas, I thought of them as discrete ideas with each one alone applying to a specific situation. The next circumstance is clearly a blend of many of your different thoughts.

As vice president, I was responsible for a department in the career and technical education area with two full-time faculty members and a curriculum that had not been updated for decades. What made it even worse was that it was an industry that had changed dramatically over the last ten years and there were good employment opportunities for program graduates with state-of-the-art skills. The faculty were very "experienced" and they were not hostile to my suggestions for change, but nothing ever happened. It was classic passive-aggressive behavior. They seemed content to keep doing what they had always done and not have to do all of the work necessary to revise the program. I knew that the path of least resistance was to not fight the situation and either let the program die or wait until they retired. However, as we discussed, I knew that I could not be satisfied with the status quo, particularly because it was hurting their students. I also thought that if I tried more dramatic measures, I would open myself to criticism and failure. Nevertheless, I decided to take the risk of trying to make a change through more significant actions than just persuasion.

I did not inherit any negative evaluations for the faculty involved so taking the necessary actions to terminate them seemed possible but lengthy. So, I tried the old "work around". I used some of our very limited resources to hire a new full-time faculty member even though it was not justified by the enrollments. The person hired was current and knew what skills program graduates needed to be successfully employed. I also promised the new faculty member an equipment budget to implement some of the changes he felt were critical. A year later he left because he was totally frustrated. The senior faculty either blocked or undermined his attempts to change the program. I viewed my attempts as a failure and it haunted me – both because I hate failing and I was unhappy about wasting the resources. Eventually, I disbanded the program and reassigned the two faculty to other departments in which they were eligible to teach. The expectations placed on them by the faculty in those areas probably were the main reason for accelerating their date of retirement. Besides the disappointment of eliminating a program that could have been viable for students, it also made me cautious about attacking other weak programs. I continued to clean up other programs but it was always with more fear. Grandpa, can you think of how I could have handled this differently?

Well, we have all been there and we have all had similar experiences. Each of us has a certain naiveté which causes us to believe we can fix any problem or, as teachers, reach every student. Not all problems are fixable or require too much money and energy to fix them. As I became more seasoned, I made the calculation about when to proceed with trying to change something and when to mitigate against it causing negative consequences. However, in the situation you described, doing nothing was never a viable option. You appropriately decided that you would not accept the status quo. So, we need to start by redefining failure. Failure was to do nothing. You did not fail because you resolved the situation; it was just not your most desired outcome. We have to be very careful about ever labeling something as a failure because of precisely the consequence you described. Fortunately, it didn't keep you from making other necessary changes but I have certainly seen that happen. I hope your president reinforced that belief and did not ever provide you with a negative comment because the first effort did not work.

This may sound strange, but I think your course of action was correct. I think you should try to save a viable program before you disband it. However, remember you cannot force people to change; you can only encourage them to change themselves. The one difference I might suggest is that I learned when trying to make these types of changes, a critical mass helps to make the change happen. At a minimum, you needed two new faculty so that they can work together and support each other while trying to overcome the resistance to change. Even when they are in the minority, two people will be far more successful in making changes. However, in some departments that are larger, it will take even more and in all cases require administrative support. I know this would have meant taking an even greater risk, but it became my guide because one person alone always seems doomed unless he or she can convert the existing faculty. That usually never happens or the existing faculty would have responded to your suggestions in the first place. If that had happened, you could have given them one person to help implement the change but not to initiate the change.

The other recognition I developed over time is that you receive much more "bang for your buck" by giving additional resources to successful programs rather than failing ones. In the beginning, out of an effort to be fair, I spread the new resources in some equitable manner. Unfortunately, without some other type of intervention, failing programs did not improve. So, in the absence of other criteria, I always tried to support winners and reward success.

Thanks for the reassurance and the ideas of how to handle future situations like this one. I particularly like the ideas of obtaining a critical mass and backing winners.

Grandpa, I wanted to talk with you about "Creating Oz" – setting aside time to work on the big ideas. I certainly understand why it is important. Also, I understand the concept of needing to set aside the time for working on these big ideas or I would never get around to doing it. Nevertheless, the gap between understanding all of this and doing it is enormous. My previous supervisors, including my current president, were always focused on current institutional problems and pressing me to work on them. I have never found any of them committed to working on the big ideas if it was at the expense of spending time on solving current problems. Perhaps it was because of pressure from the Board of Trustees, but I have always been given the impression by them that focusing on the big ideas was a waste of time given the number of challenges that the college was currently facing.

Beyond that, all of my evaluation systems have focused on short-term re-sults with no recognition of long-term planning or problem solving. I think that is also true for the president's current evaluation by the board. Because of the immediacy of current problems and the systems for prioritizing work, there is no priority within our current organization for working on the big, long-term issues. As a result, it was hard for me to make it a priority. If that wasn't enough, I have had trouble controlling my calendar because of the demands for me to be present at meetings and to meet with individuals on campus. I have also noticed, because my door is always open, that people who just drop in seem to feel that if you are spending the time thinking or writing, you are not busy and can be interrupted. So, you can see why I feel that I have not been spending very much time working on the big ideas, but I still feel it is important and I want that to change in my new job. Do you have any suggestions?

Well, it should be easier to change the value system of the organization when you are the president because you will have more control over the institutional systems. I would begin by talking with the board about your evaluation and the importance of having a long-term component. If the board starts to have it as an element in your evaluation, they will also start to pay attention to it. Of course, you have the ability to incorporate a comparable element in the evaluation processes for all of your senior administrators. I would also suggest that you meet with the faculty leaders about how to create an institutional dialogue among employees on these issues. Faculty are usually willing to engage in these discussion if they can see a purpose. That will be up to you to demonstrate that the college will act on mean-ingful outcomes. Those are some ideas off the top of my head for how to change the culture of the college.

Beyond that, you need to find some methods for carving out your own time without closing yourself off from the people in the college. In other words, don't start closing the door and say that you cannot be interrupted. Instead, find a way to do your thinking outside of the office. I often did some of my best thinking while going on walks alone. So, I would schedule walks in which part of the time was my walk around campus talking with people and part of the time was to go off on a walk by myself. These walk times were scheduled and held as much priority as any other meeting. People seemed to be very accepting of the practice because many of them had seen and interacted with me during a portion of the walk. I also carried paper and a pen for making notes on the big ideas as well as items I learned during my walks on campus.

Beyond the walks, I found a place on campus outside of my office where I could go to write. For me, it was at a study booth in the corner of the library. Not only did everyone leave me alone because they could not find me (and if they did, I discovered that writing in a library is perceived to be serious work) but I also frequently had a chance to interact with students. The other time that is available is at the beginning and end of the day. I always worked long hours and it was usually quiet before 8:00 in the morning and after 6:00 in the evening. While I could have used this time for working on the big ideas, I usually used it to handle emails and other operating responsibilities so that I was available to talk with people during the day.

Thanks, grandpa that is a big help. I had not thought about first changing the college culture in my new job before I try to use your suggestions for carving out my own time for working on the big issues.

You know, out all of the advice and suggestions you have given me, I probably generated the most mileage out of the idea to "build as many named partnerships as possible". It is something that I have continually developed in every job and, if anything, I imagine I will do even more as a college president. I have been very fortunate to have supervisors (especially my current president) who gave me great freedom and authority to develop partnerships, and I want to be sure to do the same, on a selective basis, when I am the college president.

I wanted to describe a couple of them for you so that you can see how I have taken your advice to heart. The first example was between the college and a local land developer. The developer had acquired land adjacent to the college for the purpose of building condominiums. He had received all of the necessary permits and he had even received from my predecessor an easement on our property (for what I must say was a very small amount of money). The developer's land was on a hillside and required excavation to create a building pad for a large part of the development. In order to create the pad, the developer needed to construct a 60 foot high retaining wall on our property line with the wall being anchored on our property using the easement. We all agreed it would be ugly and pose a potential hazard (especially if children ever climbed up near the top of the wall to drop objects for fun and either caused damage from the falling object or one of them fell).

I approached them with the idea of working together to find a better solution that would benefit both of us. What I suggested was that, instead of building the retaining wall, why not have the developer come onto our property and terrace the slope. The depth necessary for terracing was roughly equivalent to the depth of the easement which the college was already prohibited from using within the terms of the easement. So we were not giving up any land. They would perform the terracing, plant the terraces and maintain it in perpetuity. Therefore, we accomplished the same purpose as the retaining wall without building it. Obviously, the easement was no longer necessary and could be eliminated and we both had a much more attractive buffer between us.

But the real sweetener was yet to come. I demonstrated to them that this solution would save them an enormous amount of money by not having to build the retaining wall and that we should participate in that savings. It was agreed that they would make a donation to our foundation for $500,000 as an element in the deal. I felt this was a great win-win partnership with an unlikely partner and showed me that it would always be worth the effort to partner with others to find mutually beneficial solutions. They received a more attractive solution, eliminated a potential hazard and saved money (even after making the donation). We also got a more attractive solution and our largest unrestricted donation to the foundation.

Let me also tell you about another partnership that was very different but was equally successful in a very different way. The partnership really involved our college and two other parties. The first party was a large private foundation with a very supportive foundation president. He had read about our college in the newspaper and wanted to help us. The foundation ended up helping in many different ways, but I want to focus on this one particular aspect of our relationship. I explained that in addition to money, I could also use their help in gaining access to major universities to form potential partnerships. For a long time the private foundation had been providing funds to some of the most prestigious research universities in the country. In response to my request, the president of the foundation arranged for me to meet with the president of one of these universities. The university president was very friendly and cooperative (probably because he did not want to offend one of his major donors); but after we spent time together, he became committed to creating a meaningful partnership between our college and his university.

His university had a preeminent interdisciplinary, neuroscience institute. He proposed that we select 3 – 5 of our best biology students and 3 – 5 of our best psychology students to serve as summer interns at the institute performing primary research under the direction of their faculty. Since the university was some distance from our college, students would be provided

with free room and board, as well as a stipend for their work. The founda-
tion was so intrigued with the idea that it agreed to fund it. The experi-
mental partnership was a great success and has existed for over a decade.
It provided an incredible experience for this select group of lower division
undergraduate students (an opportunity that was not even provided to the
university's own lower division students). However, the performance of our
students provided an added benefit. The students performed so well that
the university faculty looked forward to having them and never thought of
it as a burden or "charity". We even had some of the university faculty state
that some of our students had outperformed their own graduate students.
This resulted in the other benefit of creating a very positive image among top
research university faculty about the abilities of community college students
in general and about our students in particular.

> Those partnerships are incredible and certainly take
> my suggestion beyond my wildest expectations. What
> is even more impressive is that you said these are just
> examples of many partnerships. You certainly must
> have made your college proud by your efforts, and
> one of these days I would like to hear about the oth-
> er partnerships. Besides being great partnerships,
> they also demonstrate the importance of the leader
> continually looking for ways to partner and to being
> open to all kinds of new relationships. I don't think
> either of these would have happened if you had not
> approached these opportunities with that mindset.
> You did a great job.

I don't know about you, grandpa, but I am getting stiff from sitting here
so long and my coffee is ice cold. How about we walk to a little store I know
that is nearby so we can stretch our legs? Better yet, when we reach the store
we can have some fresh coffee; and while there is not much in the store to
buy, they have great pieces of homemade dark chocolate.

I would never say no to fresh coffee and dark chocolate. Let's do it!

Grandpa and I made the quarter-of-a-mile walk to the store
and talked about everything other than work. We had spent so
much time so far discussing leadership issues that both of us felt
the need for a break. However, it had been so long since grandpa
and I had been able to have these lengthy discussions, I was relieved to discover that we could pick up where we left off. The one
difference was that now I felt we talked about these issues as professional colleagues and that grandpa clearly saw me as a professional
peer.

When we arrived at the store, we were pleased to see that they
had just brewed a pot of fresh coffee and that the dark chocolate
chunks had just been made that morning. After making our pur-
chases, we slowly walked back to the park while sipping our coffee
and eating the chocolate. There is nothing like sugar and caffeine
to reenergize us.

*I want to change gears, grandpa, and talk about some of my experi-
ences as they relate to your "Oscar and Emmy Awards of Leadership"
list. I understood the lessons of "Sanford and Son". And, I had no
problem applying the lesson of telling the people I hired and the people
who directly worked for me how to do their job and how I wanted it done
in terms of the managerial or technical parts of their job. However, I
had great difficulty explaining to those in leadership roles how to be an
effective leader. It seemed as if the people who were successful by and
large came to the role already possessing most of the necessary leadership
skills or a predisposition for developing those skills. I was certainly able
to help them fine tune those skills but the suggestions and changes were
modest. On the other hand, those who came to the job lacking funda-
mental leadership ability never seemed to get it, no matter what I said
or did. Of course, I was not able to spend much time with them; so that
may have also contributed to the problem. As I think about it, it may not*

be just a distinction between those who had the skills prior to their new job and those who did not, but rather a distinction between those who were like sponges soaking up and applying all the sources of improvement and those who remained clueless.

I particularly noticed this difference among department chairs – probably because it was the first real professional leadership position for many of them. I had two department chairs who especially had this problem. They were always coming to me and needing me to solve problems that I expected a department chair to solve. Even after coaching them, I inevitably had to go in and resolve the situation. I would always suggest that they watch how I handled it and maybe that would help them in the future. However, nothing seemed to matter. A new difficult situation would arise and they would be right back in my office. What could I have done differently to help them become effective leaders?

You may think I have the answer to all questions, but in this case I don't know. We talked about this a little when we took our walk in the botanical garden but we did not directly answer the question of how to transform a non-leader into a leader. I am not sure that I ever successfully did it either. It is a critical question that I will try to think about and give you some answer before I go home.

In the short run, those individuals probably need to be replaced as department chairs. This is often hard because they are elected, and you don't have the authority to simply remove them. Nevertheless, either talking to them and convincing them to resign or trying to have the faculty within the department make the change may be your only options. In the case of the latter, it will not happen unless you stop rescuing the ineffective department chairs.

As you move up the administrative ladder, we have to make the tough recognition that not everyone is capable of doing these jobs. Even if we knew how to make everyone a successful leader, which we clearly do not, you do not have the time to spend with them that would be necessary for the conversion. You have to reach the conclusion that right now the individual is not the right person for the job and you need to make a change. This will become even more critical when you have the authority as the president to make those changes in administrative positions. Good people can be a bad fit but an organization can only prosper with the right people performing each of the jobs. It is not a pleasant part of the job but a necessary one.

I suppose that provides the perfect transition to my sharing with you some of my experiences relating to your "Carol Burnett Show Emmy" advice, in particular, surrounding myself with great people and being a caring person. I must say, I have wrestled with this situation in every leadership position. I never underestimated the importance of hiring and selecting the right people. So, I always gave a lot of time to the selection process and never treated it in a casual manner. Nevertheless, I still occasionally made mistakes by selecting the wrong person, or it was out of my hands because I inherited someone who was the wrong person for the job. That leads to the hard part – ending the employment of your mistakes and the inherited problems while being a caring person.

My first experience occurred as a department chair with a full-time probationary faculty member who was in a tenure-track position. The entire faculty involved in evaluating him felt he was either poor or mediocre and that, as a department, we should not grant tenure for mediocre, or worse, performance. They were also all very "caring" people who did not want to offend or confront their colleague, so they all gave him satisfactory

evaluations. I was the only one who gave him an unsatisfactory evalua-
tion. Still, each of these evaluators came to me and in private said that we
should not grant him tenure. Accordingly, I started the process to end his
employment at the end of the academic year. As you might expect, he fought
it and said that I was the only one who felt that way and used his evalua-
tions from the others as evidence. Fortunately, I prevailed with the college
vice president and president so the process continued, but he requested a
final hearing before the Board of Trustees. About two hours before the hear-
ing, one of the faculty evaluators came forward and substantiated my deci-
sion and indicated that it was supported by the faculty in the department.
In the face of her statement, he resigned. However, he still continued to
teach in the department until the end of that semester!

As a result of this experience, I learned a number of important lessons.
First, once it was over, I knew I had done the right thing and the depart-
ment was better as a result of my actions. I even realized that I could do a
better job as department chair with him gone. Second, I realized the impor-
tant role that the president played in backing me – both because he believed
in me and because he was vehemently committed to the college not granting
tenure to mediocre performers. Third, I learned a hard lesson in peer review
by caring people. In all future evaluation situations involving peer review,
I always recounted this problem (in general terms) and required from each
evaluator the commitment that they were prepared to make the tough recom-
mendations if the situation called for it. Just going through this exercise
requiring personal commitments made an enormous difference in all future
situations, and I excused anyone who felt they could not make the commit-
ment. Fourth, I learned that no matter how unpleasant it is to perform this
task, once you have reached the decision, don't delay. Take the action and
get it behind you but do not ever relent by accepting mediocrity. Like others
in our profession, I am also a caring person so this was never easy; and
it was even more difficult when the person being denied tenure was a very
nice person. However, I realized it is a necessary part of the job. Because I
wanted everyone to be successful, I always continued to start out by doing
everything possible to support people and help them. But, I also know that

you reach a critical point where you cross a threshold and need to begin preparing to make the tough decision.

Just as you suggested, I learned that having the right people (at every level) surrounding you creates the optimum work environment. It obviously increased my performance and the performance of our organizational unit. But most important, it was more fun to wake up and come to work every day.

You have clearly fully absorbed this concept, and it will stick with you forever because you have also recognized the positive consequences along with the pain. Like you, I never liked doing it. But also like you, I never backed down from trying to do what I thought was right even though I had to experience the personal pain of being the point person in these situations. The same is true with other unpleasant actions – like discontinuing an academic program or student service. With very few exceptions, everyone dislikes doing this part of the job. So don't be surprised if what you experienced as department chair repeats itself. Even superiors who support your decision are glad to have you be the one to actually perform the termination and have the confrontation with the employees and their supporters.

Now that I am leaving the college to assume the presidency, I wanted to tell you that your advice from the "Mr. Holland's Opus Oscar" was right. All the time that you are working, you are never sure whether you are appreciated. However, now that I am leaving the college, I have received wonderful notes, emails and in-person comments in which people told me how much they appreciated my accomplishments in my various jobs, but what was really noticed was the way I performed my jobs. You were right in that people did notice my caring and acts of kindness and hard work. Unfortunately, I was unable to hear it until I was ready to leave.

I think that is the way of the world. You should consider yourself lucky because you at least heard it. Most people go their whole life without hearing that praise and appreciation because unfortunately most of us don't tell people and then it is too late. We need to tell people on a continuous basis and not wait until they leave or die.

On a lighter note, I will give you a more humorous version of learning that people are watching to see how hard you are working. There was a time in my career in which I walked to work (although most people did not know it) and I just left my car at work (in my dedicated parking space). I worked very long hours so people always saw me around but a concern started to develop that I was working too hard and people were worried about my health. A small group came to talk to me about this and they said, "We know you work long hours but we feel it is out of control. No matter what time any of us arrive in the morning and no matter how late any of us work, your car is always here and you are always working." After laughing and telling them how much I appreciated their concern, I confessed to walking to work. Yet, it certainly made me realize how closely my behavior was watched.

Grandpa, probably the advice that has been the most difficult for me to fully internalize has been the message of the Cuckoo's Nest Oscar. I understood what you were saying about ½ of 1% of any group causes the problems and are probably emotionally disturbed. However, their comments were often personal and they hurt. I have had a very hard time compartmentalizing comments from this group and accepting that they are based on

misinformation and intentional efforts to create conflict. I can even intel-
lectually understand that some of their personal attacks are really aimed at
my position and not aimed at me as a person. It is just very hard not to feel
the pain that they inflict.

Besides the personal attacks, there are also the problems created by the
disruptions they create and the time spent trying to remedy them. I have
not been able to simply ignore their demands and I continually try to find
some compromise solution with them. Of course, in many cases, even when
I find a solution, it does not last. It is just a matter of time until they are
back with a new issue.

I wish I could I give you an easy solution but I don't
have one. As I told you during our walk at the fort,
I also had the same problem. I tried to play the old
axiom in my head that "you cannot please all of the
people all of the time". That is especially true when
you appropriately are trying to keep making changes. For some reason, many of these types of conflicts
are out of a desire to go back to some point in the
past. Worse yet, if you acquiesce to their demands
in order to avoid conflict, you are not leading in a
manner that is in the best interest of the college. In
many ways, it is like our earlier conversation about
terminating employees. It is not pleasant; but if it is
not done, the college suffers. In this case, the college
will suffer if you give in. The unfortunate part of this
situation, unlike the employment situation, is that it
will continue to go on for a long time, not just a set
time period.

In terms of the personal attacks, I think it is important to discuss it with your superiors or, in the case
of your new job, with the Board of Trustees and your

colleagues. While you cannot keep people from ex-
pressing their opinions, you can demand civility, and
it is easier if it is done by someone who is not under
direct attack. Unfortunately, many of these people
will make the attacks behind your back and not directly to you. If they are confronted, they will deny
it. Nevertheless, if the people surrounding you know
that you are always trying to create an environment
of civility, they will call these people on their comments even when you are not present. Just be sure
that you are always working to create civility and
don't allow others to be personally attacked. Every
effort to move discussions out of the personal and
towards a discussion of alternative approaches to a
problem will help with your leadership, especially
outside of the ½ of 1%, even if it doesn't solve the
problem with this group.

*I know I have bombarded you today with all of these experiences, and I
appreciate your willingness to listen to them all but, if you can stand it, I
have one more.*

Sure. The coffee and chocolate gave me some more
energy. I am glad we had that enormous brunch today before we left for the park. Actually, none of that
matters because I cherish this time with you discussing professional matters.

*Thanks, and I also love this time together. My last one is really about
all of your advice and my experiences as a total group. It is the message of
the "Music Man Oscar" listing in which you discussed the importance of
leadership traits needing to be internalized. I must admit that it was not
easy to internalize all of your suggested traits, and I wanted to let you know*

what worked for me. As I said earlier, I have always had the "Wizard of Oz" list as well as the "Oscar and Emmy" list posted in my office where I could continually look at them. However, just looking at them did not internalize the traits. What worked was that having them so readily available kept them in my consciousness and slowly, through a variety of experiences, I was able to apply or use them. It was through this application in my actual experiences that the internalization started to occur. With each success (and even some of the failures), the trait was reinforced (or I recognized the problem was created by not doing what you suggested), and the use of the trait gradually became second nature to me. For me, anyway, it seemed to require this combination of being aware of the trait or skill and the application of it in my actual experiences.

I might add that, beyond the great advice I have received from you, you will notice that on the lists I have added my own notes and my own awards. These additions are of a more personal nature and based on my own observations. I have never really had a single mentor (with the possible exception of you, grandpa) but I have learned positive and negative lessons from all of my supervisors and colleagues. Watching others perform really has helped me to grow as a leader.

I think your observations are wonderful. Everything I shared with you has been a retrospective. I have been reflecting on what I did that worked but you have actually chronicled your growth as a leader. I think your idea of knowing what to do, combined with the experiences of applying the ideas, is the necessary combination – both for internalizing the traits and growing as a leader. I am also thrilled that you have gone beyond our discussions to personalize the ideas to fit your needs and style of leadership.

I am glad you shared all of these experiences with me, but I hope you realize that the "Wizard of Oz" list and the "Oscar and Emmy Award" list will be just as useful in your role as president as they have been in your previous leadership roles. I hope you will continue to use and show all of the traits that have made you so successful to date. People should not change their leadership style as they assume leadership roles of greater responsibility, but they do need to understand that every job is different and requires new skills. You cannot act in your role as president in a manner identical to the way you acted as vice president. You are now at the top where "the buck stops" and that requires different behaviors than the ones you used to support your current president. Of course, you have had to make similar changes as you moved from department chair to dean to vice president but the move to president is quite different. Now that you are going to assume the presidency, I hope we will have the chance to talk about some other thoughts I have had since we had those walks 15 years ago.

I have really enjoyed today and I am looking forward to spending more time with you during our stay, but I feel I have reached my limit for one day. I hope you don't mind, but I need to call it quits for today.

I hope I didn't talk your ears off and I am ready to stop as well. Let's go see how grandma is doing.

8

"A Walk to Remember"

At breakfast a few days later, grandpa said, "I enjoyed our conversation the other day and it really energized me. Ever since we talked I have been thinking about my time as president of the college. It has been a long time since I visited the college and I would really like to see it again. In particular, I have not seen all of the new buildings and renovations that we planned while I was at the college. Would you mind if we had our next talk while we walked around the college."

I quickly agreed. After all these years, we had never really been present at the college at the same time. I was proud to be his granddaughter, and I was proud of my accomplishments at the college, so I thought it would be fun to walk around together – seeing the college through the eyes of the past and the present. In particular, I wanted him to see that his dreams for the campus really had come true.

While we were driving to the college, grandpa said, "I appreciate that you are always on time." He admitted that people who were late were one of his pet peeves. Grandpa said that, through his entire life, he always tried to be on time or early; and it was particularly true during his professional career. When he was in charge of a meeting, he tried to start on time out of respect for those who showed up on time. People who are late are saying (probably unintended) that their time is more valuable than that of the other people in the meeting. By starting on time, the message is clearly given that it is up to the late attendees to determine what they missed from those who were on time.

We arrived at the college and had just started our walk down the primary campus walkway when I was approached by a member of the faculty. He wanted to know if I could make a room change for one of his classes in the fall semester, and I agreed. After he left, grandpa asked, "How are you so sure that you could make the change so late in the process?" I said that I was not certain I could but I would try my best to make the change. He reminded me that I had not qualified my response and that the faculty member probably thought it was a done deal. Grandpa said, "I know you responded in a way that you felt sounded receptive to his concern and inferred that you would make an effort."

"However," he said, "while the specific situation is not important, I learned through my own mistakes that it is important for leaders to remember that they should not promise (or imply a promise) unless they know they can keep it. This situation was minor and if you cannot keep it, you can probably talk to him and explain how you did your best but why it was not possible. Yet, the next time you answer a query with certainty, he now knows that it only means maybe and that your answer cannot be completely trusted. He undoubtedly knows it is not intentional, but there may come a time in which he will not make a reciprocal commitment because he knows he cannot trust your answer. I know this may feel like I making too big of a deal out of this lack of clarification, but it is these little things that, I learned the hard way, help or hurt your image of honesty and transparency. In listening to myself, I realize that I sound a bit 'preachy'. You probably don't need that kind of advice anymore but like being on time, it was another of my peeves when people make promises that they can't or don't keep. I am sorry for getting on my soapbox, and I will try to constrain myself in the future."

I laughed and told grandpa, "Don't worry about it. Even though I have been chosen to be a college president, I still want all of the help and advice that you have always given to me – even when it comes from a soapbox!"

I am not sure if I was relieved or disappointed that, when I introduced grandpa to the member of the faculty, there was no recognition of him being the former president of the college. It did not take long for that to change. We went in to see the new Student Services building and we immediately ran into one of grandpa's former colleagues who was also having a tour of the new building. The two of them enjoyed an extended period of reminiscing, and then grandpa excused himself. While I waited for grandpa, his friend pulled me aside to tell me something. He said, "What made your grandpa wonderful was no matter how many accomplishments occurred under his leadership, he never took sole credit for them. He always gave credit to others for their contributions and when describing the accomplishments, unlike many of his predecessors, he always used the pronoun "we" instead of "I". More importantly, he did that, not because it was some leadership gimmick, but because he genuinely believed that the accomplishments were the result of the efforts of many people, not just him. As you might guess, because we were all included in receiving credit for our successes, it just made us work harder to help him." When grandpa came back, he said his good-byes, and we continued our tour of the Student Services building.

At the end of the tour, we went by the room in which an orientation session was being conducted for first-time students who would be starting college in the fall. Much to my delight, the woman conducting the session called me in and asked me to offer a greeting to the new students. While I fumbled around for a few seconds, I eventually talked briefly about the college and I welcomed them. When I came back to meet grandpa in the hall, he had a smile and asked how it went. I explained that I was fine once I started.

He shared with me a little "trick" that he had developed over the years for just these types of situations. In particular, he said, "When I was president I was frequently called on to speak without being given any notice. So, I carried in my pocket a brief note with five talking points on college subjects that were my highest priority at that time. In that way, I was always prepared and I always used the moment to its greatest advantage."

He also said, "As leaders, we should not underestimate the importance of these impromptu remarks. For many of the people in those audiences, it may be the only time they hear you speak or the only time this year. Just think about those new students. How many of them will ever hear you speak again? They will form their impression of you based on those remarks you just made. The same is true in every audience. If you are prepared, people will at least judge you as competent and knowledgeable. Depending on your delivery, they will also make judgments about whether you are approachable and seem nice (as opposed to arrogant or belligerent)."

Grandpa said that because of these impromptu presentations, "I also came to realize the importance of how I performed at all-college meetings (like the one prior to the fall semester). This was especially true when I was president." Grandpa said, "I came to realize that for a significant percentage of the employees of the college, it was their primary exposure to me and that they would judge me on the basis of that performance. It also set the tone for the year and my leadership style, which is why I always tried to be optimistic, positive, hopeful and uplifting while still being honest and transparent. It will be particularly important for you this fall when you speak at your first all-college meeting at your new college." At this point we decided to leave the building and explore the rest of the campus.

We spent the next hour wandering all over the campus. Grandpa was thrilled to see the improvements that had been made since he retired and how closely the changes reflected the master plan that had been developed during his time at the college. He remarked about how he often worried when these plans were developed, whether they would be followed or just collect dust on the shelf. In this case, he was excited that the plans had actually been followed. Grandpa also enjoyed seeing a few people who were still at the college from his time and he relished being caught up on what they had been doing.

Grandpa indicated he was ready to stop and rest so we walked over to the "Coffee Stop" where he ordered his Americano coffee and a chocolate chip cookie. As we sat outside under an umbrella, grandpa reminisced about how much he always enjoyed when he was president going for walks around the campus.

> I know we touched on this the other day when we were talking in the park but now that we are back at the college I am reminded about how important it was to me. First, I could see what was happening and I was not dependent on others for conveying it. It meant I was not so isolated and I could learn what was really going on at the college. Second, I could talk to people in their space as opposed to them having to come talk to me in my office. Most people will not want to bother you, especially if they are happy and have nothing to complain about. Third, I will hear many more positive comments when I walk around than I will ever hear in my office. As a result, it helps you to maintain a better personal balance. Fourth, it was only by walking around that I ever had the chance to talk to students. Finally, just the

physical movement of walking, instead of just sitting
at a desk, always made me feel better.

For all of these reasons, he tried to regularly walk the campus,
even if it meant scheduling it on his calendar.

The ancillary lesson to the importance of walking around is
that when you are in the office, whenever possible, leave the door
open. There are a group of people who will formally schedule ap-
pointments to see you. However, many of the employees do not
want to make it so formal and want to be able to just drop in and
see if you have a moment to talk with them. Grandpa said, "I always wanted to be accessible to those individuals." Many leaders
complain that they cannot get any work done during the day if the
door is left open. However, grandpa's theory was to try to get that
type of work done early in the morning or in the evening so that
the day was free to meet and work with other people. It meant for
long days, but he always felt that came with the job.

We finished our walk in my office on campus. As soon as we arrived, I was approached by one of the faculty members who asked
if I had decided yet on whether to proceed with the new program
that he had proposed. I told him that I had not yet reached a decision and that I was still trying to collect more information regarding the proposed program's viability. After he left, grandpa
remarked that this was always a tough call as to when you did not
have enough information to make a decision and when you were
needlessly delaying the decision by collecting more information.

Clearly you want to operate by making data driven
decisions but you also recognize that you will never have enough information to insure certainty of
making the right decision. It always ends up being
a judgment call that seems to be a function of the
personality of the decision maker. The "cowboy"

doesn't collect enough information and just acts on gut instinct. The "deer in the headlights" cannot ever make a decision and always wants more information. Each of us has to decide where we fall on that spectrum and hopefully we make decisions as quickly as possible with at least the minimum necessary information.

Grandpa and I decided it was time to leave so we could stop on the way home to eat lunch. However, before we left, grandpa thought he should stop by the president's office so he could pay his respects. The current president is someone he knows but only through very casual contact. He is not someone grandpa ever worked with directly before he retired. After exchanging pleasantries, the president said that he was glad we stopped by because he was planning to call grandpa. The president has decided that he wants to hold a series of workshops for all college leaders and he wanted grandpa to use his experience to make presentations for two of the workshops – one on leadership strategies for public community colleges and one on long-term issues facing public community colleges. Grandpa said, "I might be a little rusty, but I am thrilled to be asked and I would be glad to do it." We then said our good-byes and left.

I was glad that I had brought grandpa to the college for our talk. Not only had our walk allowed him to reconnect with the college, but it also prompted him to give me a number of "tips" that he might not otherwise have remembered. While they were all helpful, I particularly liked the five ideas in his pocket, remembering that he was always being judged, the "we not I" idea, the importance of walking around and keeping the door open.

On the way home, I could tell that grandpa had already started thinking about the presentations, and I began to think about what it would be like to be a participant in one of grandpa's workshops.

Of course, I guess this is the next logical sequence in our time together. I have had my private tutorials, and now I would join others as a member of the audience.

The next day, I tried to think about how I could remember his leadership "tips" from yesterday. I decided to create the Post-It shown below and stick it on my computer monitor when I moved to my new office. In that way, I could keep reminding myself to use his suggestions.

STRATEGY POST-IT
- Be timely
- Promise what you can deliver
- "We" instead of "I"
- Pocket list of 5 talking points
- All public speaking is important
- Go walk around
- Keep the door open
- Decide with data, but decide

❖

9

Leading a Successful Climb

I arrived about five minutes early to the room where grandpa's seminar was being held and found that the room was almost filled. The participants ranged from department chairs to the college president, but also included leaders from the academic senate and the collective bargaining units. Most of the fifty or so people in the room did not personally know grandpa, but they knew about him and his work at the college. As a result, there was a certain air of anticipation in the room.

I also wanted to be sure that I could remember everything grandpa said so I recorded the lecture and diligently took notes. Based on those materials, I have tried to capture the essence of the presentation.

The president of the college opened the session by stating, "I believe that being a leader is a continuous learning process so that all of us need to keep working at being better leaders." He continued by saying, "I think it is also important to learn from the people who preceded us and had been successful during their tenure." The president finished his introduction by providing a brief biography of grandpa and said that he certainly fit the characteristics he was looking for when he was seeking potential facilitators for these leadership seminars.

True to form, grandpa began with some self-deprecating humor and some funny observations about how the college has changed since he retired. I knew grandpa was nervous because, while he used to do public presentations all of the time when he was at the college, in retirement speaking in front of groups had become a rarity. Nevertheless, the humor put the audience and grandpa at ease so that he quickly resumed his relaxed form.

Grandpa continued by saying he did not want any misunderstanding about today's discussion of "Leadership Strategies for Public Community Colleges".

> In a two-hour session I cannot provide an exhaustive discussion of all the critical strategies and there are excellent alternative presentations on many of them, such as strategic plan development, financial strategies, accreditation issues, human resources, use of technology, and specific strategy development within academic and student affairs. I am not going to provide any in-depth discussion on student success measures, outcome accountability and many other topics. I know that all of these are important subjects that everyone needs to understand, but instead I want to talk about eleven specific leadership strategies that were foundation strategies for me and which cut across everything else.

The first two strategies relate to how a leader constructs the decision-making environment with the people in the organization (no matter if it is the entire college or a single department). He said, "I have always been a believer that **educational organizations work best when they utilize a well-defined and committed form**

of participative management," Unfortunately efforts to use participative management have struggled in many settings because too many leaders and too many participants did not have a solid understanding or acceptance of how it should work.

It begins with the leader and a commitment to the principle that involving others in decision-making actually produces better decisions. A successful model also requires the establishment of a relationship between the leader and the participants in which there is an environment of mutual respect and trust. For example, a college president must have this relationship with the vice presidents but must also have that same relationship with faculty and staff leaders, including collective bargaining leaders. It is also critical that these same people understand the boundaries and responsibilities of being a participant in this relationship. A successful use of participative management cannot happen instantly. Understanding the roles and building the mutual respect and trust requires time and shared experiences.

Participative management is not a democracy, it is not a town hall vote and it is not delegation of authority to a committee. Instead, it is an open and frank discussion of situations and possible solutions in which the leader and the participants contribute ideas and actively listen to others in the group. In the case of the president, he or she will still be held responsible for the decision and, as a result, must retain the authority to make the decision. However, the involvement of others cannot be a charade. When it works well, there is frequently concurrence on the decision or at least a full understanding of why a particular decision was made in the absence of concurrence. It is equally important that participants understand their responsibilities beyond the direct participation. Specifically, participants are expected to communicate with their followers so that an understanding of the process, and as appropriate, an understanding of the decision percolates down through the organization. It also means at times that participants must keep confidential information to themselves even though it is tempting to share it!

The second strategy that grandpa discussed was that, as much as possible, **decision-making processes should be data driven**. He admitted that this is a two-edged sword. On one hand, if participants can agree ahead of time on the data elements for a decision, the data tends to drive everyone to a common solution. It also tends to remove the emotion from the decision and not make the decision appear to be subjective. As a result, data-driven decisions create rational decisions that more readily gain support of people within the organization. On the other hand, data-driven decision-making processes can create two forms of consternation. Some leaders resist such a decision-making process because they feel it erodes their authority and their ability to make decisions using more variables than just those produced by the data. That is an accurate concern but can be overcome if there is a positive working relationship between the leader and the other participants in a participative decision-making process so that it is understood that data is not the exclusive determinant of a decision. The other problem is that people who don't like the decision attack the data – either the data is inaccurate or the wrong data was utilized. That is why it is critical to agree on the data elements before the outcomes are known.

> One final comment on both of these strategies is that many leaders and participants pay lip service to being believers in participative management and data-driven decisions, but when it comes down to it, they are not committed to the principles. On the part of leaders, the usual problem is an unwillingness to share any element of their authority to a collaborative process or to data. Instead, in their heart, they want absolute authority and the ability

to make whatever decision they want to make. In the case of participants, they howl when the decision is contrary to their wishes. Either they fail to accept the principle that it was always the leader's place to make the decision (not a vote of the group) or they object to the data elements because the data did not produce their desired outcome. That is why both of these strategies require the development of a genuine commitment on the part of everyone.

The third strategy is more controversial and is certainly not the consensus among successful leaders but is a strategy that grandpa said he has always believed in during his career. It is the strategy that **a college must always continue to market an image of quality and always grow the enrollment demand for the college**.

As you might guess, everyone subscribes to this principle when funds are abundant and when growth is being funded. The controversy comes when that is not the case. When funds are being cut and/or growth is not funded, many colleges cut the marketing and outreach budgets because they do not believe they are a priority in that environment.

Grandpa said he disagreed. A college that has a well-developed, continually reinforced image as a quality institution creates for itself a "Teflon shield". When the public thinks of the college as a place of excellence, and bad things happen, they dismiss those things as anomalies. However, if a college has a negative image, and the same things happen, those things reinforce the public's negative image of the college.

The difficulty is that a college must continually work to build and sustain a positive image. It is not an effort which can be turned on and off or only done when there is an abundance of resources. As academics, we often find it hard to accept the reality that the public forms an impression of the college based on very little information (maybe without ever setting foot on the college) and they repeat that impression by word of mouth. That is why the effort needs to be continuous, and when funds are limited, it is better to initiate programs that don't require money or do fewer quality promotions than it is to do promotions of lower quality.

A similar logic also applies to growing enrollment. In our society, colleges must grow to prosper and most systems financially reward growth. When those rewards are temporarily suspended due to difficult financial times, it is still beneficial to build up demand so that it can be captured when the rewards return. When a college turns off the "enrollment spigot," it is often hard to turn it back on quickly. As a result, there is a financial opportunity to generate the enrollment when other colleges cannot do it right away. If the financial constraints are so serious that a college cannot continue to build (or sustain) demand, the college must have developed a specific plan as to how they will quickly grow the enrollment when it is once again funded. Otherwise, the resources will go to those who can respond quickly.

In addition, even during the times in which enrollment growth is not rewarded, there is a reason to still use recruitment efforts. First, it levels the playing field among potential students. In the absence of college efforts, there is a bimodal distribution among potential students regarding the knowledge about how to gain access to limited enrollment slots. Recruitment efforts close that gap by helping those students who come from families without college experience and knowledge about "how to play the game". Second, creating unmet demand makes the college seem more desirable, which in turn makes those who are admitted feel better about attending the college. It also increases the attractiveness and interest of more students who have alternatives (presumably better prepared students). This "creaming effect" is thought to improve college outcomes which in turn will attract even more students. Right or wrong, and in spite of statements to the contrary, people in our society feel bigger is better and will eventually reward size. If the college now matches this growth effort with an equal commitment to student success and positive student outcomes, and markets those results, "the world will beat a path to its door".

The fourth strategy relates to a technique grandpa said he learned when he had to promote the college without funds. He hired a former journalism instructor to help him, and together they worked extremely hard to **develop a positive relationship with the major daily newspapers in the area**. Since his predecessor refused to talk with the newspapers, it made it easier for him to gain access. The creation of a positive relationship began by agreeing with the primary reporter from each paper that he would return all phone calls either the same day, if possible, or within 24 hours. The college also readily welcomed in-person interviews and on-campus access. Beyond the reporters, grandpa met periodically with the editorial boards of the papers so that initially they knew what he was going to try to do and later, they were given progress reports.

The first benefit from this relationship is that the newspapers always contacted the college before writing any negative articles (contact had stopped happening in the previous era) so that in some cases the college demonstrated that the situation was misrepresented and the article did not appear. In other cases, it resulted in a balanced presentation so that the college could at least have its side fairly represented. However, the second benefit was more important. The college developed success stories; and in most cases, the newspaper printed some version of them. Some of the stories were of a human interest nature that portrayed the successes of particular students. In other cases, it was reports on student outcomes and student success at the college. Both helped to develop the college with the desired image of excellence. Furthermore, by having the reports in the newspapers, an element of credibility and third-party objectivity was created so that it had a much greater impact on the public and potential students. Grandpa said the college even enhanced the impact by having the articles reproduced and distributed at feeder high schools – all done at very little cost to the college.

Related to these strategies, grandpa always felt it was critically important to **direct the college's primary focus on feeder high school students** (although not to the exclusion of other potential student populations). Feeder high school students are the primary source of full-time students which is at the core of the college and are often the eventual returning students after a hiatus from education following high school graduation. However, it was also his belief that high school students were the primary basis for word-of-mouth references to the college. These references were usually based on relatively little information, making it critical for the college to influence the student perceptions of the college. High school students are readily defined and reachable with very little waste of marketing dollars so that the college gets its best "bang for the buck". Finally, it appeared that differentiation between the college and other local competitors among parents was being defined by their children which in turn led to parent word-of-mouth references to the college. When the marketing dollars were limited, grandpa always focused on the feeder high schools.

The fifth strategy is marketing related but from a different perspective. **Appearance of the college matters**. Potential students, community members and donors frequently make a judgment about the college simply based on how it looks. By appearance, grandpa said he did not mean that the college needed to be fully composed of new buildings, but rather what mattered was how the college was tended. Are the building exteriors freshly painted? What is the condition of the landscaping around and between buildings? Are the interiors of the buildings clean? If one thinks about how people visit a college without being a student, this all makes sense. They walk around campus and mostly just see building exteriors and the landscaping. If they go in a building, it is usually just the main corridor. Of course, they may also use the rest rooms – particularly in certain areas of the college. Based on these visual impressions, they will make a judgment about the quality of the institution. There will also be an extensive part of the community that will never come on campus and will base their impression on the exterior of the college. Again, there is an assumption that if it looks good from the street, it must be a good place. The other part of this judgment by impression will be how people on campus interact with them. If the employees and students are helpful and friendly, visitors assume it is a welcoming college that cares about its students. If not, it creates the opposite impression.

Maintaining college appearance in hard times is a real challenge for the leaders of the college. When funds are short, the classic response is to cut custodians and gardeners while also postponing deferred maintenance. Furthermore, if areas of the college are understaffed, workers can be overloaded and "grouchy". However, if the college community believes in the importance of college appearance to visitors, there are low-cost solutions. What is important is that leaders work to maintain the appearance, even if it means watering and mowing weeds or using court workers and community volunteers. Even the strategic planting of flowers can be a low cost, effective improvement of appearance. Where there is a leader commitment, there is a way to achieve it, and when it is achieved, the result is that it also raises the morale of current employees and current students.

Grandpa said the sixth strategy seems so obvious that it should not need to be stated but yet it does. Colleges exist for the benefit of students, and leaders need to **build colleges around meeting student needs and achieving student goals**. In many cases it does not need to be done at the expense of meeting employee needs (administrator, faculty and staff), but when employee needs are not reconcilable with meeting student needs, the college must make students the priority. Probably the most obvious neglect of this strategy in colleges is the schedule of classes. How many colleges create schedules that offer classes that the faculty want to teach instead of classes that students need? Or, how many colleges offer classes at times and in locations that fit the faculty needs instead of when or where it would be best for the most students? Or, how many college services are operated (or staffed) based on the times that are most desirable for the employees rather than students? Or, how many decisions are made to bolster the egos or reputations of college leaders or trustees? No segment of a college is immune from this problem which is why particular attention needs to be paid to placing students first when assessing the outcomes of decisions, especially during difficult financial times.

A by-product of the sixth strategy is the seventh strategy. **The biggest contributor to cost control is maintaining (or building) the average class size of the college**. This does not mean creating class sizes that are inappropriately large. Instead, it means that once class sizes are determined based on academic appropriateness, the college should make every effort to make sure there are not empty seats within these parameters. The most common cause of the "empty seat problem" is what was mentioned in the previous strategy – the wrong classes being offered or the right classes being offered at the wrong time. Because faculty usually develop the schedule of classes (or at least the initial draft), maintaining average class size requires continual vigilance. It is not because of malicious intent by faculty but, in the absence of thoughtful review, schedules of classes tend to migrate into offerings that best serve faculty needs and not necessarily student needs.

However, enrollment recruitment is also a factor in maintaining average class size. When the college creates unmet demand, students will take classes at less desirable times and from less attractive teachers because it is better to have some classes, rather than none. Filling empty seats in the schedule of classes is perhaps one of the most critical factors in the financial health of the college but is often given inadequate attention. Grandpa finished his discussion of this strategy by saying that the financial impact of increasing average class size by 10% is amazing.

While talking about the financial health of a college, grandpa said that his eighth strategy is **creating an environment in which saving money is rewarded** (or at least not punished). Too many colleges base subsequent year budgets on prior year expenditures which punishes budget centers that spend less than they were budgeted and rewards centers that spent their entire budget. Colleges need to find ways to reward savings and, if possible, allow departments to spend their savings in future years or at a minimum does not decrease their budget because they did not spend it all. If a college does not reward savings, departments will be sure to spend their entire budget each year and stockpile supplies and other items. Saving funds also needs to be encouraged at the college level. Leaders should commit to a minimum reserve requirement and agree that all funds saved in excess will be used in the following year to better the college. It is simply operating the college on the old consumer wisdom of "save the money first and then buy the item". If this philosophy can become part of the college culture, people realize that it is the means to obtain a new staff position or new equipment which would not be possible to fund out of a department's own budget. It also makes everyone feel better when the funds can be used for such items as campus beautification or improvements in food service or other common needs.

The ninth strategy is based on the **recognition that public community colleges operate in a political environment**. Generally speaking, community colleges are political assets to elected officials so be sure that they know about the college and that you provide them with "good news" items that they can use in public appearances. At the same time, when bad things happen (especially if they will make the news), be sure to inform elected officials of the details (ahead of time if possible). The greatest dislike of an elected official is to be surprised, which in this case, is to be asked about a problem for the first time in a public forum. Usually, elected officials want to be supportive, but that is only possible if you give them the details. When doing it, be honest or they won't trust you when you describe a problem to them in the future. It also helps if you can give them some idea as to who will contact them or what they will be asked.

Grandpa admitted that good communication can be time consuming but he said that one of his best decisions was to hire on a part-time basis one of his political science teachers (who had experience working for elected officials) to help him. One of the successful ideas from that person was to organize periodic group breakfast meetings between the president and the chief staff member from each elected official's office. It would have been impossible to bring all the elected officials in the same room at the same time on a regular basis, but it was possible with their staff members. As a result, a rapport was developed with the staff members (which helped in emergencies), but they were also prepared to keep the elected officials apprised of what was happening at the college. Besides, grandpa felt they also appreciated being recognized as playing an important role on their own and not just as an appendage to the elected official.

The tenth strategy is really one of correcting a myth. Many leaders believe that people and foundations give to the neediest of institutions but grandpa disagreed. He felt that **donors gave to winners or those that had the prospect of being a winner**. It is a simple concept but when asking for money, don't plead poverty or describe how needy the college might be. Instead, describe the greatness of the college and even how much greater it would be if you had their contribution. Besides, the employees and students like being portrayed as winners. Every college needs to be on a path to greatness.

The final strategy that grandpa discussed was the **importance of putting this all together into a coherent, understood message**. Everyone within the organization needs to understand where the leader is trying to go and how he or she plans to get there. Some people call this a vision and others think of it as a strategic plan. The name is less important than the purpose. People within the organization need to feel they are being led because they understand where the organization is going. In that way, everyone can participate and "row in the same direction".

The leader also needs to have a well-thought-out, integrated plan so that he or she acts in a way that is consistent with past actions and consistent with what he or she has said. There is nothing more discouraging to an organization than having a feeling that the actions of leaders are aimless and that the organization is adrift. While it is important to have a plan, it should not be handcuffs. The plan needs to be continually revisited and revised as conditions change. Also, when opportunities present themselves, they need to be acted on even when they were not part of the plan. Just don't forget to explain the changes and deviations.

Grandpa finished the session by saying that a strong leader has a well-defined vision and plan that everyone knows and understands. He said, "It was my plan to end this session after two hours and, since I only have two minutes left, I am stopping." However, before he left, he reminded everyone that there would be one more session next week, at the same time in the same room, in which we would look at perpetual community college issues that never seem to be resolved.

By the way, I should mention that yesterday, when grandpa and I were at the mall, he ran into an old college friend. While they were catching up on the intervening years, it was apparent that their professional lives had taken very different paths. Grandpa spent his career in education and his friend spent his career in the private sector. Nevertheless, they found points of commonality and grandpa had invited him to today's lecture. Since he did not know anyone in the audience, I invited him to sit next to me. I am mentioning all of this because at the end of the lecture, I happened to notice his notes and asked for a copy. They are interesting because grandpa's friend clearly saw the parallel between grandpa's experience in education and his experience in the private sector. Here are his notes:

Success Strategy Notes

- In most work environments, a participative management style that creates participative decision-making works best.

❖

- Data-driven decisions create thoughtful decisions.

❖

- Always market a quality image of the enterprise and continually promote reasoned growth.

❖

- Always maintain good relationships with your core group of clients.

❖

- Appearance matters.

❖

- Ideally, an enterprise exists for the benefit of its clients.

❖

- Pay attention to productivity for it is the key to cost control.

❖

- Reward financial stewardship by employees.

❖

- Remember that all ventures operate in a political environment.

❖

- People want to associate with winners and potential winners.

❖

- It's critical to have a core vision that everyone understands and embraces.

10

Widening the Trail

When the college leadership group gathered again the following week, there was still a feeling of anticipation about the session, but the tension had been replaced by a feeling of familiarity. Having spent two hours together the previous week, both grandpa and the group felt they now knew each other. Beyond the previous week's positive experience, the feeling in the room was probably enhanced by the fact that grandpa brought coffee, tea and a wide variety of chocolate pastries for everyone. Nothing like coffee and sugar-laced food to bring a group together!

I know from last week that grandpa's presentation today would be filled with information that I would want to recall and use. And so, I asked our college to record his presentation and I came prepared to take extensive and detailed notes. Using those aids, I have tried to recreate grandpa's second lecture.

Just like last week, the president introduced the session. He obviously felt no need to introduce grandpa, so after thanking everyone for coming, he went straight to today's topic – long-term issues facing community colleges. The president said that when he and grandpa talked about these leadership seminars, they agreed that one of the sessions should focus on generic long-term issues that face all community colleges. The president went on to say that he and grandpa agreed that an important part of being a leader is to work on issues that transcend a person's immediate leadership responsibilities. Too many leaders only focus on their college and their current or short-term issues. Since both the president and grandpa have had long careers in community college education, they also recognized that there was a subset of these long-term issues that never seem to be solved or go away. It is those issues that we will focus on today.

Grandpa greeted everyone by saying that it was great to be back for a second week. He confirmed the remarks of the president by saying that they both were struck by how persistent some of these issues were and that some of them not only continued through grandpa's 40-year career but that he thought some of the problems were issues for community colleges when he was a high school student. However, grandpa did not want to overemphasize the historical reference or try to prove in every case that the issue has existed for 50 years but instead to simply use the recognition that these concerns did not just happen and they wouldn't be solved quickly.

Because of the longevity of the issues, "I will also not be able to give you easy answers. If I knew the answers, I would have solved the problems. As leaders, it is easy to become involved in the mundane or short-term problems while ignoring the big issues." Grandpa said, though, "If the leaders don't spend time thinking about these big, persistent issues, they will never be solved. Even though the answers won't be easy, we need to keep working on these concerns. You may not feel that you can make a difference on these issues, but you can. By spending time thinking about these problems, you might be the one to develop the solution. However, if you just insure that these matters are discussed at the college, solutions might be found at the local level that could be replicated at the system level. Even if that does not happen, if every college is talking about these challenges, it will result in the profession and the systems devoting time to working on solutions." Given our time limitations, grandpa said, "I am going to focus on just six issues. You should know that these are my opinions, the issues I think are most important. But they are based on my 40 years of experience."

The first issue, and probably the most persistent issue, is **the public perception that public community colleges provide a lower quality of education than the lower division of undergraduate programs at public four-year colleges and universities. This is in direct contradiction to the evidence.**

Community colleges have smaller class sizes. The faculty academic preparation is comparable to the professional faculty at other institutions. No classes are taught by teaching assistants (unlike many universities); and, in fact, many community college instructors developed their skills as teaching assistants while attending graduate school at a university. It wasn't until those skills were perfected that they became teachers at a community college. Many community college faculty also teach, or have taught, at universities. Community college faculty have chosen teaching over research. As a result, they have no research requirements, and they do not view their teaching responsibilities as interfering with their research work (in many universities research is the basis of faculty evaluation and the granting of tenure). Accordingly, there are numerous testimonials by students who transferred to the university about the superior quality of the teaching they received at a community college. Most people who have experienced lower division education at both a community college and a university would not argue with the belief that the level of instruction provided by the faculty at a community college is superior.

So, grandpa said, "If it is not the teaching at a community college, what causes the image problem?" He felt that it was exclusively derived from the difference in the admission criteria. In

California, for example, the University of California is supposed to take the top 12 ½ percent, the California State Universities are supposed to take the top third and community colleges are supposed to admit anyone 18 years of age or older or anyone with a high school diploma. The tuition is also tiered in relationship to the admission standards. The public assumes that if it is harder to be admitted, the institution must be of a higher quality. Presumably, lawmakers agree, which is why the tuition correlates with the admission standards.

The corollary to this argument is that the competition in the classroom is much tougher when the admission standards are tougher, so therefore a student receives a higher quality of instruction. However, community college transfer students perform in their junior and senior years in a manner equivalent to students who started as freshmen at the university, so the community college students were not handicapped by the competition. Also, all of the transferable community college courses were articulated with the universities so that the content and standards are comparable. Furthermore, there is no notable GPA deterioration among transfer students between lower division work at a community college and upper division work at a university.

One of the notable differences among the higher education segments is the "success rate". Of course, this is probably a function of the admission standards and the level of student preparedness upon entry. If a comparison is made of an institution that essentially accepts everyone to an institution that only accepts the top 12 ½ percent, the success rates should be different. However, success rates are probably comparable for comparable student populations. Nevertheless, the difference in "success rates" (however that is defined) causes community colleges to receive much greater scrutiny in the public policy arena and unfair publicity about their success rates which reinforces this false public perception about the quality of education in a community college.

If the public were rational, why wouldn't everyone go to a community college for two years and then transfer to the university of their choice? It would cost less money; and, at a minimum, a student would receive a comparable education (probably superior). It is an issue of irrational status that is perpetuated by all segments of society. High school principals and faculty create a report card for themselves that documents how many students they send to each segment with a higher grade being earned for sending the greatest number to the institutions with the toughest admission standards. High school students with choices are always encouraged to attend the institution with the toughest standards which creates a community college image of being a place one attends when you have no alternatives. Too often no one suggests that if you attended a community college and saved money on the first two years, it would help to pay for upper division or graduate school. It would be the rational decision; and if one enrolls in an honors program, it would even parallel the student competition of a university. What is even more tragic are those instances in which students attend universities directly out of high school and are forced to incur large student loans to pay for the cost of lower division classes when there was a low-cost, high-quality alternative in community colleges.

Students also balk at going to their local community college because it means they live at home and continue to go to school with many of the same people they knew in high school. Of course, it means students save the cost of room and board; but if that is not an issue, students could easily avoid these concerns by attending a community college outside of their immediate community. There are many alternatives in all of the urban and suburban communities which are even commutable, but it is also possible to move to another area as the student would need to do to attend a university.

Grandpa also offered one other aspect of this issue and that is the portrayal of community colleges by the media. Whether it is a standup comedian or a weekly situation comedy, the community college student is almost always portrayed as not being very smart and not being very serious. Again, it perpetuates the image problem for community colleges. It would be nice if once in awhile the media mentioned how many high school valedictorians have attended community colleges.

The second issue is the **financial structure for public higher education**, especially community colleges. It is reasonable to assume that colleges will plan for oscillations in their revenues, like any other public or private organization. In particular, that means that colleges will maintain adequate reserves to assist during difficult times. If the college has adequate reserves and appropriate financial plans in place, the economically difficult times are only a severe problem when they persist for more than three years. The reason that longer term solutions are a problem is that, in many cases, the college cannot change its revenue stream since the college does not have taxing authority and cannot set its rate of tuition. These situations are particularly problematic when colleges are financially operated as state institutions and revenue streams are dependent on state-level decisions.

To many, the solution seems simple. If you have less revenue from the state, serve fewer students. Unfortunately, for most colleges that solution does not even work at the financial level, because the marginal cost savings from enrollment reductions is less than the decline in marginal revenue. Many colleges (and legislators) operate on the assumption that revenue streams will be maintained at the total cost of education per student when, in fact, revenues occur at a marginal rate per student that is lower than the total cost of education per student. As a result, it is assumed that a reduction in marginal revenue can be offset by a corresponding percentage reduction in enrollment. That is not true. When "the public" (by voting on specific measures or by acts of the legislature) decides it does not want to maintain funding for community colleges, the only viable escape valve is to raise alternative revenue or decrease access in a manner that will result in a reduction in expenditures that directly correlates with the reduction in revenue. Too often, the allowable reductions in access are too small and colleges are forced to reduce quality for the remaining students.

The "public" needs to understand that revenue reductions mean fewer students will be served and the allowable access reductions must be large enough to permit colleges to maintain the same level of quality for the students who will be served. In the case of alternative revenues, that gap is too often filled by simply raising student tuition. Grandpa said, "We will come back to that problem in a minute because both raising tuition and lowering enrollments clearly cause an access problem and force colleges to not fulfill their stated mission. Traditionally, colleges have not allocated the reduced access but simply served students on a first-come, first served basis with an ability to pay the tuition. Is that the proper response or should there be a more deliberate allocation of the access? " A systemic solution needs to be developed to sustain colleges during an economic downturn of more than three years while at the same time assuring that colleges can be self-sustaining for the first three years through proper financial plans, use of reserves and modest student fee increases.

A solution for revenue declines beyond three years will probably require identifying a dedicated revenue source that does not change as a direct correlation with the economic cycle. Of course, when revenue streams increase, those dedicated revenue reserves need to be replenished. Likewise, when revenues increase, colleges must be prepared to grow enrollments, replenish college reserves and lower tuitions. Sadly, in many cases that does not happen.

Even if we can solve this problem, there is a bigger systemic financial problem. Community colleges have an inverse relationship between enrollment demand and the economic cycle. Student enrollment demand increases as unemployment increases. It is logical that people want to be retrained, or additionally trained, when they lose their job. Society also needs that training to take place to help reverse the economic downturn. Unfortunately, just as this increased enrollment demand is occurring, college revenues are being cut which means enrollment is being reduced. Not only is enrollment being reduced, but frequently the targets of those enrollment cuts are the more expensive career and technical education training programs that provide the necessary instruction for the unemployed. Since this cycle seems to always repeat itself, grandpa said, "We need systemic plans for its occurrence. We meet those demands in wartime, we should plan for comparable solutions during peacetime economic downturns."

The third persistent issue is **access**. With the increase in technology and the knowledge base, some postsecondary education has become critical to acquiring and sustaining livable wage jobs. For openers, that means it is not acceptable to simply maintain the adult participation rate in postsecondary education. The rate must be increased if, as a society, we are going to maintain acceptable employment levels and continue to make progress as a leader among developed nations. That means beyond all other barriers, the seats must be available for those who are trying to go to college.

Of course, even if the seats are available, there are financial barriers to attending college. Often the focus is on tuition as the critical financial variable. While the amount of the tuition can be a barrier, it is probably not the only critical factor for many students. The necessary support materials (textbooks, instructional materials, computers, etc.) often exceed the tuition – especially in community colleges. However, for students who must work to support themselves or their families, the cost of not working to attend school is the real burden. If they cut back on their work hours, how will they pay for food, housing, clothes, transportation, etc.? Given the limitations on financial aid, students become caught in a "catch 22" in which they cannot afford to reduce their hours, but if they only go to school outside their work hours, they must take a very limited number of courses (or risk being unsuccessful in their courses by taking too many courses as a part-time student). Even this can be a strain because of child care concerns and the time to degree when only taking one or two classes per semester (this latter problem is particularly exacerbated if the student must finish developmental work in math and/or English prior to taking college courses).

This problem is particularly acute among the working poor who may be holding two minimum-wage jobs to make ends meet. Here is a group of people with a very high work ethic, working 60 to 80 hours per week, but are caught in a vicious cycle. They cannot work fewer hours to go to school to gain the skills for a livable-wage job because they cannot survive on less income. At the same time, if they don't obtain the skills, they are locked into being part of the working poor for the rest of their lives. The business community states that above all else they value potential employees with a strong work ethic. This working poor population seems ripe for attention in which we capitalize on that work ethic by giving them the critical skills to gain livable-wage jobs.

Higher education is primarily a passive system. That is, we serve those who show up at our door. It means that all those members of the population who don't seek postsecondary education are ignored. Just as we don't count among the unemployed those people who have given up and stopped looking for employment, as a society we don't worry about trying to serve people who are not actively seeking a college education. As grandpa just mentioned, that group certainly includes a large portion of the working poor. However, there is a more startling concern. Large urban communities have a large population of "youth" (between the ages of 16 and 24) who are not working or going to school (estimated at over 100,000 in Los Angeles alone). Most of these individuals are unskilled, and many of them never graduated from high school. If educational institutions don't engage these individuals, convince them of the importance of being educated and educate them, it will reduce the available work force and they will become a social liability. Right now, these potential students are not even on the radar screen.

Grandpa continued to say that when talking about access, educators need to think of it in the broadest terms because being educated and having an educated populace has become a critical variable in individual success as well as the social and economic success of society. This increased need is occurring at the same time as a general belief that individuals need to pay a bigger share of their postsecondary education with less of it being subsidized by government agencies. When these two concepts collide, the number of available seats is reduced and the tuition is increased. The existing financial barriers become even larger and there is no social desire to increase adult participation rates or to embrace new populations within college attendance. Grandpa said he worries about the future if a solution to this issue cannot be found.

The fourth issue is the **preoccupation by external agencies on student success**. Grandpa said that throughout his entire career he never worked at an institution that was not concerned with student success and utilized internal measures independent (or inclusive) of those imposed by external agencies. It is not a new issue, and it will never be resolved because colleges will always work to improve student outcomes. A significant part of the debate over the years has focused on how to measure student success and how to compare success measures at different colleges given the disparities in student populations and service area populations at those colleges. Unfortunately, more effort is spent on defending, creating, disputing, etc., the measures than is spent on improving student success. To resolve that dilemma, an honest discussion about external preoccupation with the measures needs to occur. Is it to punish poor performers? Is it to punish community colleges in general? Is it based on a belief that public resources are being wasted because of too much attrition? Or, is it to find models of excellence so that the success can be repeated in other places? Presumably, if everyone wants to improve student success, this needs to be a collaborative effort, not a competition. If that is to happen, those same external, evaluative agencies need to help create that environment of cooperation.

Related to improving student success, institutions and systems need to decide what price they are willing to pay to improve student success measures. Many educators believe that students should have the right to fail so that we should advise but not restrict students. Others believe that reasonable restrictions should be in place to help insure student success. Where this plays out is in the areas of mandatory assessment, mandatory enrollment in developmental skills courses if indicated by assessment, and skill prerequisites (or advisories) on college-level courses. Whatever the decision, there is no perfect answer, and so there is a price to pay. There is also a financial price to pay.

Many "boutique" programs have shown great success, but they are very expensive to offer on a large-scale basis. At some level this includes intervention programs (e.g. EOPS, Freshman Experience, finding the student fit between motivation and goal, mentoring) and new developmental skills approaches, but at the other end it involves programs such as internships, university experiences prior to transfer, authentic job placement and genuine partnerships with employers. Beyond this financial price, there is a third price to pay – a willingness to make radical change in education. Educators need to look at how we teach. There has been no significant change in centuries. Instruction is still reading dependent. Is that the best way to continue when current students are so much more visual and auditory learners than previous generations? Grandpa said he was not suggesting the solution but encouraging the investigation and using current students as partners in the exercise.

The other related issue for postsecondary student success is whether it is time to blur the distinctions between K-12 and postsecondary education. Everyone agrees that learning is a continuum and that the current distinction is an arbitrary boundary that was created for administrative purposes. Wonderful efforts to create a "college experience" for better prepared students (e.g. Advanced Placement, Running Start in Washington and similar programs in other states) have been developed. There have also been greater efforts to start assessing college readiness in the 11th grade, but it is again primarily aimed for the betterment of the well-prepared students. Success has been achieved through creating middle college high schools. The education system just needs to keep pushing those boundaries. Similar efforts need to be made in the area of developmental skills for those assessed as not being college ready and advanced placement (or college enrollment) for 11th and 12th graders wanting to complete workforce development programs. Besides helping to keep students engaged and stimulated, the system would optimize the use of time and reduce the time to degree for all students. This may be one of the solutions to the financial barrier to access.

The fifth issue is perhaps more esoteric but is one that is continually debated. **What is the optimum method of organizing colleges and what is the optimum size of a college?** Are the issues related? Is it best for a college to operate as a single entity? Does it have to be a certain size in order to capture economies of scale and breadth of offerings? Does a college become dysfunctional if it is too large? When should a college develop multiple campuses of the same college? When should they become separate colleges? Should small colleges bind together? Everyone agrees there are benefits from being a large college (or district) that range from economies of scale to political influence. Everyone also agrees that at some size the organization becomes dysfunctional. There are also benefits of being large enough to offer a full spectrum of programs and services which makes a college more desirable to prospective students, but at some size the college loses the nurturing aspect of treating students as special individuals.

In all organizations, there is the debate about appropriate centralization and decentralization of decision making, but that debate is particularly fervent in multi-campus and multi-college organizations. No one has determined the optimum answer to these questions. Grandpa said that there is no single answer but a set of variables that must be satisfied for each structure and size, but no one has delineated those variables. As a result, community colleges have no uniformity of organization or size and no conditions for each that must be met. Without these answers, the results are predictable – success and failure simultaneously for every size and organization structure. Grandpa said this is one persistent issue which should be resolvable through a thorough investigation of each success and failure. Maybe the answer is not a structural question but dependent on the leadership of the institution. Now all that has to be done is to find the time to do that investigation!

The final issue that grandpa discussed was **whether community colleges had responsibilities beyond fulfillment of their educational mission**. Clearly public colleges were built with public funds and, as a result, the public needs to have access to those resources, but not without limits. The funds were committed for the purpose of education, so community access should never interfere with the college fulfilling its primary mission, and providing the access should not divert funds from the primary mission. In essence, the community access has to be at no cost to the college. However, beyond casual, individual access, a college receives numerous requests for continuous scheduled facility use (particularly athletic facilities). Again, these requests should not interfere with college functions, but for these types of uses, a financial contribution to the college needs to be made. If for no other reason, the planned repetitive facility use by a single community organization locks out other public uses.

Of course, beyond access to college facilities, the college needs to be a community resource for intellectual and cultural pursuits. The community needs to be an active audience for the arts, athletics, and general access programs in other areas of the college. At times a college can seem to be a nuisance to immediate neighbors (e.g. traffic) so whenever possible it helps for the community to perceive the college as a welcomed resource. The issue is defining the boundaries. There are always more things a college can do for the community, but they must be balanced against the cost – not just the direct cost but also the cost in terms of the time and energy spent by college employees. This struggle can at times be exacerbated by elected college trustees and other elected officials who are eager to please members of the community. Grandpa said it becomes even more difficult when the request involves access to politicians and advocacy groups. As much as possible, these boundaries need to be established before the request so that the leader's decision is the enforcement of a policy and not one of trying to write a policy in the face of a request.

Beyond these types of regular requests, there is also the issue of whether a college has the responsibility to provide examples of a model community. Especially in urban and suburban areas, colleges usually have over 10,000 students. As such, they are the size of many villages and towns. Given the knowledge base and social awareness in a college, should the college provide experimentation in collective actions that could be replicated in other public settings? Should these models only be pursued (like the aforementioned access) if they do not divert funds from pursuit of the educational mission? Of course, when a college is looking at a model such as alternative energy sources or being a green college, it becomes difficult to define the net cost because of the initial investment compared to the reduced operating costs over time. Nevertheless, should it only be pursued if, over time, it is at zero net cost? Or should some level of cost be allowed in order to provide a model and also to be a community leader?

The other issue is that once a threshold is crossed, what are the limits? Are there financial limits? How does a college decide which models to pursue because it cannot be all things to all people? This becomes a difficult problem when members of the college community and the community at large have different priorities so while one wants a sustainability model, another one wants a health-nutrition-fitness model. There may also be models that are the clear responsibility of an academic institution, such as civility in discussing competing ideas and beliefs.

Grandpa said he was raising the issue of college responsibilities beyond the primary education mission with the leadership group because this issue tends to transcend the regular decision-making process and, if not thought out in advance, can totally disrupt a college.

Grandpa thanked everyone for their attention and involvement in his presentations but more importantly he thanked them for inviting him back to talk on these subjects. He said, "Sometimes, as a retiree, I miss not being actively engaged with a college and I sometimes feel forgotten." It was reassuring to him to see that he had not been forgotten and that people still wanted to hear his thoughts on these subjects. Grandpa said, "As you might guess, I have many more opinions and ideas on solving these problems but to discuss them would have required a semester-long course. Besides, I just wanted to get you thinking about these issues." The president of the college closed the session by presenting grandpa with a jar of mixed chocolate candy and a bottle of red wine. Clearly grandpa had not been forgotten!

$$\diamond$$

11

Grandpa's Trail

Shortly after grandpa's second leadership session at the college, he told me how much he enjoyed doing the two sessions and how impressed he was with my colleagues and the state of the college. However, grandpa said, "I feel our discussions are incomplete because I have one more set of topics that I want to talk about with you before you start your new job." Since I was trying to finish my current job and start visiting my new college, I asked grandpa if we could take one more walk on Saturday. He agreed and I knew it was important to him because he would have to miss watching his favorite team play its first game of the football season on television!

When we left for our walk, grandpa said that today he wanted to go to a place close to my house. We started by visiting a local pizza place. Grandpa ordered his half with black olives and barbecued chicken while I had onions and artichoke hearts on my half. We bought a couple of local micro-brewery beers to go with the pizza. Grandpa directed me to a trail head which was only a couple of blocks from the pizza place but led into a wonderful set of woods. With our food in hand, we started along the trail. In less than a quarter of a mile, we arrived at a picnic table perched near the top of a modest waterfall. It was a waterfall that cascaded over a series of ledges rather than having one precipitous drop. The waterfall was beautiful, the pool at the bottom of the falls was peaceful and the noise of the rushing water in the woods was a perfect backdrop for lunch and our last discussion.

Grandpa said, "I don't think our conversations would be complete without talking about the personal side of leadership. I want to talk about my own feelings about leadership from when I was doing my various jobs and as a reflection since I retired." He also said, "I might be repeating ideas today that we talked about earlier, but it would be from a different perspective. When we spoke earlier, I was trying to give you my principles of being a good leader, but today if I repeat myself it is because it was a principle that I held 'near and dear'."

> Leaders have to create a style and manner of leadership that is an honest extension of their personality and their beliefs. You cannot be an actor playing the role of a leader. You cannot learn a leadership technique and then portray that trait without it being genuine. Leadership traits must be internalized to be relevant. It is the tricky part about teaching leadership skills. People can intellectually understand the principles, but if they cannot internalize them so they become a natural part of performing as leaders, then nothing meaningful has been learned. If you cannot internalize it, don't fake it. Always be authentic as a leader. If you are not, at some point the mask will come off. When the mask comes off, it is worse than never having faked the leadership traits because people will feel cheated and manipulated, believe you are a phony, and resent it. People will respect more an honest, authentic person with weaknesses, rather than a charlatan.

Being authentic and adopting a leadership style that is an extension of your positive traits is not easy. It has to start with being able to be introspective and having sufficient self-esteem that you can identify your positive traits. Without these two ingredients, it will be difficult to be a leader. At the same time, you must be comfortable in identifying your weaknesses so that you can develop a plan as to how you will compensate for them. I felt that part of my success was that I was authentic and what you saw was what you got. I did not have different styles in different college management settings (except when there was a physical emergency).

I was fortunate because many of my personal characteristics were a good fit for being an effective leader. I was extremely competitive. It didn't matter if it was playing cribbage with my wife, Russian poker with my family, a volleyball game (when I was younger) or a swimming competition in my youth.

In all forms, grandpa admitted he always wanted to win. It meant that he always drove his organizations to win, even if only he saw it as a competition. At the same time, it also meant that he took losing hard. That drive to always win (or be the best) helped push his organizations to be excellent and not settle for mediocrity.

Next, grandpa admitted he always thought about ten steps ahead of his current actions. It did not matter if it was as mundane as gardening or going to the grocery store; he was always thinking beyond the immediate situation. Having difficulty living in the present was not helpful in maintaining peace of mind, but it was an enormous help as a leader because he always had a vision of where he was trying to take the organization. While communicating and implementing his vision probably drove his family crazy on family vacations, it helped as a leader because everyone in the organization knew where he was trying to go, why he had chosen that path and his strategy for arriving at the destination.

Grandpa went on to say he was an optimist, a glass half-full person (probably a trait he learned from his mother). It meant that he always approached everything with that same feeling of optimism, but it was genuine. He really believed that by working together, the organization could resolve any problem. Of course, part of this may have been based on self-confidence, and part of it may have been based on being competitive, but grandpa felt these only enhanced his optimistic outlook. As a result, in hindsight, he realized that he created an organizational atmosphere of hope and optimism because it was a real extension of those feelings within himself. The competitiveness, commitment to vision and optimism also meant that he was persistent in doing the things necessary for the organization to be successful.

Another trait grandpa learned from his parents was that even though at times he would be tempted, avoid saying disparaging comments about others, don't repeat gossip and don't play favorites. Grandma used to always say that grandpa was so tight lipped that he would never tell her anything, and she would have to hear her gossip from other people. She also said that during a brief time when they worked together, grandpa went so far in avoiding giving her any favoritism that she had to take the worst schedule. In both cases, grandpa said it never changed throughout his career. In fact, he said he had the ability to purge gossip from his memory and was so obsessive about avoiding favoritism that it could be a disadvantage to be his friend or a member of his family.

Grandpa went on to say that he felt he had been a really good teacher. "I did not feel that, as a teacher, I had been very entertaining or inspirational, but I did feel that I had a real ability to explain complex ideas and concepts in a way that all of my students could understand them." He felt that these strengths and weaknesses were portrayed in his leadership. He worked very hard to learn how to be funny, but being entertaining took a lot of work and nervous nights before performing. He also admitted that he was never able to develop the oratory skills to deliver truly inspirational and motivational speeches, like an evangelical minister. He wished he had that skill, but it did not happen. However, his ability to explain complex ideas in an understandable manner was enormously helpful in explaining certain conditions (e.g. state finances) and the various elements of his vision and plans. In short, he built on his strength, overcame one weakness, and worked around the other weaknesses.

Although he did not think about it at the time, in reflection, grandpa admitted he was probably somewhat of a perfectionist.

> When you can control all of the variables, this may be a desirable attribute. However, as you rise in the organization (to some extent in all positions), you realize that leadership requires reconciling conflicting responsibilities in the best interest of the institution, its employees and its students. For example, financial solvency and compliance with rules frequently work counter to educational improvement and student success. There are no perfect answers, and it is a balancing act in which you can always question whether you chose the right balance.

Grandpa felt that every leader needs to care about the people in the organization as individuals (both employees and students) and always lead with empathy and compassion. It is important to create an organization that nurtures. That does not mean a lax or lazy environment or one without responsibility, standards, goals, expectations and accountability. It means an organization that cares about people as individuals. Grandpa said he felt he always had that empathy, but the downside is that empathy makes it harder when making tough decisions. Just as a teacher, when he had to give a nice student, who tried hard, a poor grade, it was equally hard to lay off a nice employee who had not done anything wrong except to be in a job that was no longer necessary. Grandpa said his empathy for the person never kept him from making the right decision, but his caring kept him up at night before he met with the person and even after the decision had been rendered. He hoped that at least it helped him to deliver the decision to the person in a more caring manner and to find the most humane solution possible.

There was a personality trait that grandpa said caused him a problem throughout his career. He admitted that he was "thin skinned". It was not a difficulty in accepting criticism as long as it was justified and constructive. What bothered him were unjustified personal attacks. He could intellectually understand that at times critics were attacking the position, not him personally, but emotionally it was problematic because the nature of the attack was personal. Worse yet was when he had to deal with nasty and mean-spirited people who spread false rumors about him for the simple purpose of trying to gain personal advantage or an advantage in an institutional debate. What made it even worse was that it was usually done anonymously. Grandpa said he never found a solution that worked for him but at least had the good fortune of only having it happen to him a very limited number of times. He was never sure whether this sensitivity was from the injustice of the situation or his desire to be liked by others. Nevertheless, the effect was the same.

Understanding that each of us has a leadership style that is an extension of who we are as individuals was one of the things that grandpa said he wanted to talk about. He also wanted to reiterate that while that is the natural evolution, it can be modified by learning new techniques and by fully understanding ourselves. Beyond that, grandpa also wanted to talk about the personal challenges imposed by assuming leadership positions. The first challenge is trying to determine how to stay balanced (physically, spiritually, socially, emotionally) when the demands of leadership jobs "suck you dry".

> A leadership job is never done. There is always something else you can do to make your organization better and, unlike teaching, there is no end of the semester and a fresh start with a new semester. It is a continuum. How do you create space to meet all of your personal needs while doing the best possible job as a leader? There are limits and places where spending more time on the job does not make a significant difference, especially in light of the toll it takes on the leader. The challenge is discovering where those limits are for you. It will also change during your life and the life of the job because the time commitment is greater during your first years on the job when the learning curve is the steepest.

The other major challenge is dealing with frustration. Grandpa said, "The part that was always the most difficult for me was the frustration of knowing how to solve a problem or make the organization better but not being able to implement the action." Early in his career that blockage came from his superiors who were unwilling to allow him to make the change either because they were not risk takers and didn't want to gamble with a possible failure, or he was blocked for political reasons (usually involving personnel actions). Later, as he gained more authority, the blockage came from systemic sources. Often there were laws or regulations that prohibited the necessary actions. In some cases the necessary personnel changes were not possible because of the person being an elected representative or protected by employee contract rights or political influence. In virtually every case, the change eventually occurred, but the process took a significant amount of time and energy while delaying the necessary implementation of the solution.

Of course, there were other frustrations such as people in power (or influence) being irrational so that they became entrenched in positions that were either emotional, intuitive or simply "shot from the hip" but not based on any understandable reasoning that could be used to explain the decision to others within the organization. What made it frustrating was that, as a leader, he not only had to live with the decision but try to be supportive in his representation of the decision to his organizational unit (even having to explain a Board decision to the college). Grandpa said he could keep listing frustrations "but you get the idea". He said the important point is that he had to find a place in his mind in which he accepted the reality of the environment in which he worked and did not allow the obstacle to block his eventual success. The important idea is learning to live with the frustration of regulated and political systems and to find ways around the obstacle, not through it. Grandpa said that tolerance for frustration, perseverance and creativity were attributes he needed to continually nurture throughout his career.

As we finished our lunch, grandpa said that a question he often ponders, and one we discussed when we were sitting in the park after I had been named as president is why some people are leaders and others are not. He said that after thinking about this question since we talked in the park, he could break his answer into two parts. The first part is based on personal desires. Why do some people want to be leaders (or are willing to assume leadership positions) and others do not want to be the leader? The second separation has to do with ability. Why are some people good leaders and others are not (even though they wanted to be leaders)? How much of good leadership is a teachable skill and how much is a product of personality development and life experience? How much of being a good leader is being in the right fit between the leader and the environment in which he or she is trying to lead?

Grandpa said for all of his reflection, he only felt he had partial answers. In talking with people about why they did not want to assume a leadership position he heard a number of different answers: "I am not comfortable doing it, I feel that I would not be good at it, the job involves more time commitment and it is not a priority in my life compared to other uses of time, and it does not look like a rewarding (or fun) job (often the job is described in very negative terms)." Of course, if that is the case, why does anyone say yes? Again, the most common answers were: "I was talked into it by my peers, I saw the job that had been done and knew I could do it better or would do it better than the alternative choices (this is the feeling of responsibility to the organization), I enjoy being the leader, I was attracted by the rewards of the job (money, title, office), and I wanted out of my other job (e.g. someone who does not want to teach anymore but does not want to leave education)." People were always reluctant to admit the latter two reasons and usually, those people who became leaders for these reasons were not the most effective in the job. Grandpa felt that, as people embark on a new leadership job, they need to be asking themselves why they are seeking the job and will the reason create a successful match for both the person and the organization.

This discussion of why people assume leadership positions caused grandpa to digress.

It is an important question when you seek your first leadership position but it is even more important as you seek positions with ever greater responsibilities. It was my experience that the higher you were positioned in the organization, the less impact you have on individuals and the greater impact you have on systems. Also, the higher you are in the organization, the more you are held accountable for the actions of others and fewer of the items you are held accountable for are a direct result of your own actions. Furthermore, as you move up in the organization, and partly because of the aforementioned effects, jobs provide fewer intrinsic rewards and greater material and ego rewards. As a result of the movement along these three spectrums, being higher in the organization does not mean you are happier, especially if the promotion occurs at the wrong time in your career cycle. It is easier to take on new challenges when you feel you have exhausted the challenges in your current job. If you are unable to do a job, you are probably not happy. However, the opposite is not necessarily true. You can be great at a job but not be happy because the job does not provide you with the necessary intangible rewards. By the way, don't be caught in the myth that higher in the organization is better. There is a reason that the promotion pays more; otherwise many people would not accept the job!

Before we leave this subject, grandpa said he had still not answered the question about why some people are good leaders and others are not and whether all of the skills were teachable. Knowledge, experience, personality and fit all contribute to being a good leader. It is also clear that many of the skills for being a good leader can be learned. Inevitably, it requires some combination of both and the mix seems to vary by the individual. However, for some individuals, no matter how much education they receive, they simply do not have the personal attributes of an effective leader. At the other extreme, the so called "natural" is probably someone who has experienced a lifetime of leadership experience that started as a child because of personality attributes that kept thrusting them into leadership positions. They learned by doing over a whole lifetime. Certainly that experience has taught people many of the techniques and strategies we have discussed. However, more importantly, experience has taught them what grandpa called the "art of leadership".

Grandpa explained that by the "art of leadership" he meant that leaders learned through experience the judgment to know the appropriate actions for each leadership situation. Leaders are probably always leading. Even when they are in a subordinate role, they lead by helping the leader without usurping the role. The leader sees what needs to be done and helps to guide the group but does it with subtlety so that the defined leader is not threatened and there is no attempt to wrestle away the leadership role.

Perhaps one of the most common examples of the "art of leadership" is in attempting to control group processes. A leader should not try to control the group, but rather the leader should keep the group from getting out of control. This may seem like an opposite definition of the same technique, but it is not. Keeping a group from getting out of control allows full participation and creativity while still helping the group to reach an appropriate outcome. Controlling the group is moving the group to a predetermined outcome. Many people have great difficulty making this distinction and feel that the leader's role is to direct the process. Grandpa said to remember that that the leader's role is to reach the best decision and in a manner in which people accept the decision. The difference is important.

Another trait learned by experience is to achieve the appropriate balance in leadership techniques to fit each leadership situation. Grandpa said one can see how this applies to many of the leadership ideas we have discussed. For example, a leader

- learns how to delegate authority as much as possible without abdicating responsibility.

- listens and invites participation but knows when it is time to decide and act.

- says "yes" whenever possible but does not falsely mislead people.

- is hopeful and enthusiastic but is not a "Pollyanna".

- connects with people on the personal level without becoming friends.

It is finding this balance with each leadership trait in each leadership situation that is so hard. People trying to lead sometimes try so hard that they lose that balance and operate at one excess or the other. Experience makes finding this balance so much easier.

Grandpa told me that he had no doubt that I would be a successful president. What he wanted to caution me about was not letting my identity become synonymous with my job.

> Outside people (or even people inside the organization who only rarely interact with you) perceive the leader through an image that is associated with a person's title, not through a perception of who you really are as a person. The good news is that if you realize this, it will be easier to deal with negative comments that are based on this perception of the position, not the person. On the negative side, you may place too much credibility on the praise that is really just a product of the position, not you as a leader.

> Beyond that, if your identity becomes too connected to your job, your ego will interfere with your job performance – from too much time being spent on self-promotion or self-aggrandizement to over sensitivity to criticism or alternative points of view and

solutions. When leaders define themselves as people in accordance with their leadership position, it reduces their objectivity and effectiveness as a leader. By the way, it is even silly because most people have no idea what you do or the nature of your job.

Grandpa laughed and said that his children used to ask him what he did all day; and when he told them about all of the meetings with groups and individuals, they said, "Beyond talking, what do you actually do in your job?"

Grandpa said he wanted to end on what may seem to be an ironic note. "We have talked about what concepts of leadership would be helpful for you to improve performance, but I want to end our discussion with talking about leaving leadership positions." Grandpa said he left teaching as a full-time job at a time when he loved teaching. In fact he kept trying to teach at least one class through much of his administrative career. The value in that attitude is that "I never worried about being 'sent back' to being a teacher. On many days, it would have been wonderful. Because I was not afraid of leaving my leadership position, I felt immune from doing anything that I felt was improper or doing anything just to keep my job. There is enormous positive strength in operating within a leadership position with that frame of mind. I would have been equally happy being 'sent back' to a previous leadership position. I felt this attitude gave me the freedom to act with complete integrity and there were occasional times when I used that feeling to privately refuse to do something I was directed to do by a superior. By the way, in each of those cases, in the end it actually protected the superiors by keeping them from doing something they would have later regretted."

The second part of leaving is knowing when it is time to leave. The first concern is "staying too long at the fair". Many successful leaders have trouble leaving their jobs, especially at the end of their careers. Sometimes it is a reluctance to retire, sometimes it is a reluctance to start over in a new job, and sometimes it is just comfort in the current job. Grandpa said he always felt that ten years was about the maximum time that a person should stay in the same job. At the end of ten years the person has probably exhausted his or her contribution and at best he or she has become a maintainer of the status quo leader. When a leader stays beyond ten years, an organization's culture starts to stagnate and become too ingrained in a single mode of operation. Inevitably, even the image of what had been a very effective leader starts to tarnish which also means the person's legacy is tarnished.

The second concern is when the environment of the organization changes and it is no longer a good fit for the person. Grandpa said he wouldn't repeat himself because this was something we talked about during our time in the botanical garden. The third concern is leaving too soon. Grandpa said he felt it took three to five years to learn an organization and a position, depending on a person's background. Some people are so driven that they will try to move up before they have completely learned their current job. This inevitably comes back to haunt them because most leadership promotions assume a building block of knowledge.

> If you haven't adequately learned the previous job, there will come a time in which you are handicapped in your new job. Also, a thought that often escapes people who are on a rapid ascent path is that you can reach the top too quickly. Ideally, people assume their final position in the last five to ten years of their career. It means that they are close enough to retirement that they are not making decisions to keep their job because they can retire or assume

another job for a brief period of time. However, if you assume that you should not stay for more than ten years in the same position, you can exhaust that time and still be too young to retire. This is fine as long as you have a life plan, but it can also cause a person to stay in a job too long.

Almost as a signal from on high, it started to rain. We quickly gathered all of our lunch trash and raced to the car. Grandpa laughed as he got in and said, "I think that is a definite signal that I have talked too long." Without a doubt, it is also a signal of the end of summer. As we drove home, grandpa said how much he had enjoyed our time together and he hoped in some small way that his thoughts had helped prepare me for my new position. As we walked inside my house, grandpa reminded me that being a leader was a lifelong learning experience and he would always be available to me to help or to commiserate or to just listen. But most important, he said he wanted me to remember that he would always love me whatever I decided to do.

Postscript

I hope you have enjoyed the book and, if you found even one worthwhile idea from reading it, I will feel it was worth the effort. The book is a very personal expression of my ideas about leadership based on my experiences in various leadership roles. The book is not intended to be a management textbook. In the end, each of us must find our own leadership path based on who we are, our prior experiences and the circumstances surrounding our current leadership position. With luck, the book helped you to define your path.

As people who know me have probably guessed, I am represented in both grandpa and the granddaughter. This seemed like an appropriate representation for me because throughout my career I continually tried to be a teacher helping others to develop their leadership skills and a student trying to continually improve my own abilities. Also, I wanted to present my thoughts in a conversational mode, and I thought this format was better than talking to myself!

Each of the settings for the conversations represents a real location that I have walked since hiking is one of my hobbies. There are a few small photographs from those walks on the back cover.

In the book I mentioned the need to internalize traits into your leadership style, or the book was just an interesting read. As the granddaughter says, this can only happen by keeping the ideas of positive traits in front of you (as a help please use the notes at the end of the chapters, the lists in Chapters 4 and 5 and your own notes), reflecting on your own abilities, experiencing different leadership situations and working to improve by evaluating your performances. There is no "magic wand". So much of leadership development is knowing the traits of leadership you want to exhibit, continuous, honest self-appraisal, and as much varied experience in leadership as possible.

Good luck on your leadership journey. All of our systems, and especially higher education, need capable, talented leaders who can generate support for new directions and ideas, and lead their organization to those outcomes. I hope this book has helped to accomplish that for you and I would enjoy hearing any comments about the book that you would like to share with me (youngdf@ live.com).

Rocky Young

❖

Appendix

Suggested Managerial Skills

To give you a sense of what I mean by managerial skills, I am providing a partial list. This list is not exhaustive by any means but is intended to help you understand the distinction between managerial skills and the leadership skills discussed in this book. Here is the partial list of managerial skills for a CEO at a public community college:

1. Understand how your institution is financed.
   a. Know all of the state funding formulas.
      i. Attendance accounting
      ii. Apportionment calculations
      iii. Categorical funding
   b. Local property tax determinations
      i. Other local tax entitlements (e.g. parcel taxes)
   c. Tuition and student fees
      i. Local discretion vs. state mandates
   d. Formulas for budgeted revenue projections vs. actual revenue distributions
2. Know efficiency calculations.
   a. Facility use – capacity and load
   b. Average class size or contact hours per FTEF faculty
   c. Faculty load calculations
   d. Expense data - $/workload measure
3. State and local mandates – how calculated and results
   a. Full-time/Part-time faculty ratio
   b. 50% law
4. Accreditation
   a. Standards

b. How performance should be measured against the standards

c. Basis for sanctions against other colleges

d. How to remove sanctions

5. State Education Code and State Administrative Regulations

6. Union contracts

7. Human Resources

a. Federal laws (e.g. Equal Employment, Affirmative Action, Title IX, etc.)

b. Conflict resolution skills

c. Interviewing, hiring and evaluating skills

d. Progressive discipline

8. Marketing

9. Public relations

a. Public information

b. Interacting with newspapers and other media

10. Board of Trustees interaction and management

11. Knowledge of relevant political processes and how to influence the process

a. State legislature and Governor

b. State governing board

c. Local processes (e.g. EIR, land use, zoning)

d. Community groups

12. Foundation and fundraising

13. Grants administration

14. Management skills

a. Creating and administering a budget

b. Time management

c. How to run a meeting

15. Facilities

a. Local bond administration

b. State capital outlay funding

c. Contract bid and award processes

i. Alternative processes (e.g. RFP process)

16. Public speaking

17. Core information as it relates to the performance of your direct reports

Made in the USA
San Bernardino, CA
07 April 2014